MONGOLIA AND RUSSIA

MONGOLIA AND RUSSIA

Towards a Constructive Re-engagement

By

Vaishali Krishna

KALPAZ

ISBN: 978-93-5128-127-6

Price : ₹ 530

First Published, 2015

Published by

Kalpaz Publications
C-30, Satyawati Nagar
Delhi-110052
Ph. : 9212142040
E-mail: kalpaz@hotmail.com

Laser Typesetting: Gyan Print (AB-I), Delhi
Printed at: G. Print Process, Delhi

Cataloging in Publication Data—DK
Courtesy: D.K. Agencies (P) Ltd. <docinfo@dkagencies.com>

Krishna, Vaishali, author.
Mongolia and Russia : towards a constructive re-engagement / by Vaishali Krishna.
pages cm
Includes bibliographical references (pages) and index.
ISBN 9789351281276

1. Mongolia—Foreign relations—Russia. 2. Russia—Foreign relations—Mongolia. I. Title.

DDC 327.5173047 23

Contents

Preface 7
Acknowledgements 13

1. Introduction 15
2. Political Relations 35
3. Economic Co-operation 61
4. Strategic Partnership 89
5. Conclusion 107

Appendices 117
Bibliography 161
Index 171

Preface

Mongolia is a landlocked country located between two giant neighbours-Russia and China. It is bordered by Russian Siberia to the north, Inner Mongolia and Xinjiang regions of China to the West and rest of China to the east. Historical background suggests that in the seventeenth century Mongolia was trapped from both sides by the expansionist Tsarist Russia and Manchu China resulting into its final annexation by the Manchus. The Mongols, however, continued to struggle for their independence from the Manchu China and in this process they secured the help of Tsarist Russia in 1911, the same year when Manchu rule came to an end after the Chinese revolution. In the post-1911 period, Mongolia had to face the problem of securing recognition of its independent status from both the neighbours which shaped its perceptions of neighborhood and geopolitical constraints. But the situation in Mongolia between 1911 and 1921, as several scholars opine, may be described as "an international tug of war between Red and White Russians, Chinese, Japanese and its own radical elements." Finally, Mongolia became independent in 1921 after the second revolution which led to the establishment of Mongolian People's Republic in 1924, thus attaining the Mongolian statehood.

In the period aftermath the 1921 revolution, Soviet support and its recognition of Mongolia in 1924 made the latter one of the staunchest Soviet allies so much so that even adoption of Communist ideology and policies were hardly distinguishable from the USSR till the latter's collapse in 1991. During the entire period of the Cold War Soviet dominance was clearly visible in Mongolian politics, economy and society. In the western writings, Mongolia was even described as a Soviet "satellite", serving at the same time as a "buffer" by protecting critical points along the Chinese and Russian borders. It was largely due to the compulsion of Mongolia's geographical location, the expansionist designs of Japan and the absence of a strong and friendly government in China that forced Mongolia to come under Soviet umbrella. This was one of the main reasons for its continued strained relations with China.

Nevertheless, Gorbachev's policy of *glasnost* and *perestroika* and the ensuing process of reforms and restructuring in Soviet domestic and foreign policy influenced Mongolia also, which carried out its own process of reforms and restructuring through *Iltod* and *Orchilan baigalalt.* Further boost came from Gorbachev's Vladivostok initiative of 1986 for removing tension and conflict in the Asia-Pacific region, which changed the then political status of Mongolia as a "buffer" in the Sino-Soviet relations. Meanwhile, breakdown of the Soviet Union in 1991 also played a decisive role in the improvement of Mongolia's external environment in terms of its neighbourhood vis-a-vis China as well as securing a favourable position in the Asia-Pacific region. In addition, a major review of Mongolia's foreign and security policy gave way to the adoption of three major documents: Concept of National Security, Concept of Foreign Policy and Military Doctrine, the basic objectives of which are safeguarding the country's national interests. These documents basically show a departure from traditional mooring of dependence on Russia, apart from making commitments to internal changes through democratic reforms and market economy. As such, changes in the geostrategic environment surrounding Mongolia together with its open door policies gave way to its re-engagement with Russia on the new basis.

This book is based on the author's M.Phil dissertation entitled "Mongolia-Russia Relations, 1991-2000", which was submitted to Jawaharlal Nehru University in 2010. The study seeks to analyse the extent and pattern of Mongolia-Russia relations in the political, economic and strategic domains in the broader framework of the post-Cold War dynamism extending from 1991 until 2000. While not ignoring the Cold War period this study makes an objective investigation of the way in which Mongolia found itself dependent on the former Soviet Union for conducting its domestic as well as foreign policies. This sets the tone for analysing the whole gamut of relationship between the two sides in the changed scenario having arisen out of the post-Cold War realities during which the entire relationship began to witness a marked shift, i.e., based on the principle of equality not on the basis of Russian/Soviet dominance as was the case in the pre-1991 period.

The whole exercise is based on two main hypotheses, i.e., (a) revival of Mongolia's relations with Russia is largely for the economic reasons as Russian energy supplies provide the main thrust and (b) Russia's new foreign policy strategy to assert its centuries-old ties with "Greater Central Asia" is giving boost to overall development of Mongolia-Russia relations.

Furthermore, this study also makes an attempt to analyse the evolution of Russian policy towards post-Communist Mongolia, arguing that the policy has gone through three stages: a breakdown of bilateral relations, stagnation, and revival of relations. The revival of relations between the two countries began to take shape soon after Vladimir Putin took over power as Russian President in 2000. Hence, the whole bilateral relationship has been analysed in the context of a "Constructive Re-engagement", with the following aims and objectives:

1. To review the historical evolution of Mongolia-Russia relations and its impact on future relations, both during and after the Cold War period.

2. To examine the state of post-Cold War relations in the light of three stages: a breakdown of bilateral relations, stagnation and revival of relations.
3. To identify new opportunities as well as hidden dangers in Mongolia-Russia bilateral relations in the political, economic and trade fields.
4. To evaluate whether Mongolia's landlocked geography is a challenge for its national security and how Mongolia-Russia strategic partnership could ensure its security vis-à-vis China.
5. To examine whether Mongolia's future is still influenced by outside actors, particularly the actions and events of neighbouring powers: Russia and China.

While conducting this study, the focus has remained on the following questions to analyse the subject under study:

1. What circumstances led to the emergence of a new equation of "re-engagement" in Mongolia-Russia relations in the post-Cold War period?
2. What are the major regional and international issues on which the two countries have commonality of interests?
3. What are the key elements in the growing relationship between the two sides that could affect the ongoing Mongolia-China relations?
4. What are the indicators that point to Russia's role in Mongolia becoming in future similar to that of the former Soviet Union, particularly in the economic field?
5. Whether Russian assistance to the modernisation of Mongolian military was without binding to a pro-Russian alignment or treaty?

In terms of research methodology, historico-analytical and descriptive methodology has been followed while examining Mongolia's relations with Russia in political, strategic, economic and trade fields. Both the available primary sources such as government documents in the form of various treaties, agreements, Memorandum of Understandings (MoUs), speeches, statements and reports as well as secondary sources such as books, journals and newspapers etc., have been consulted. Different speeches, statements and reports concerning bilateral relations and data on trade and commerce between Mongolia and Russia available with various Mongolian Ministries have also been consulted through websites on the internet.

In order to discuss thematic issues separately this book has been divided into five chapters. The first chapter which is **Introduction** provides a background of the state of Mongolia-Russia relations in the pre-1991 period with particular focus on the period between 1921 and 1991, i.e., beginning from Soviet recognition of Mongolia's independence up to the collapse of the former USSR. Such broad contours of relationship between the two sides have been contextualised in the contemporary context. The second chapter, i.e., **Political Relations** highlights the extent and pattern of diplomatic relations between Mongolia and Russia during the period from 1991 to 2000. It also deals with exchange of high-level visits; various treaties and protocols; commonality of interests on major regional and international issues between the two sides; Russian support to Mongolia's participation in the activities of regional groupings, particularly in the North East Asia and Central Asia.

The third chapter, i.e., **Economic and Trade Co-operation** discusses the extent of bilateral trade and economic contacts between Mongolia and Russia, major sectors of Russian investments in Mongolia, various treaties and agreements concluded between the two sides in the economic and trade fields, Mongolia-Russia trade pattern including major items of imports and exports, Mongolia's reliance on Russian energy, and prospects of economic and trade cooperation between the two countries. Similarly, the fourth chapter, i.e., **Strategic Partnership** throws light on the defence co-operation between the two countries in the light of the changed post-Cold War geo-strategic environment of Mongolia, Russia's views on Mongolia's security concerns in terms of Mongolian policy of maintaining "balanced' relations with both Moscow and Beijing as well as role of Russia in ensuring Mongolia's overall strategic needs, besides helping to achieve economic security. While making concluding observations the last chapter gives an overview of a constructive re-engagement of the two countries in various spheres already discussed in previous chapters, besides exploring the prospects of overall Mongolia-Russia relations.

Dr Vaishali Krishna

Acknowledgements

This book is the culmination of long-drawn effort and in this academic journey I would like to thank many but gratitude to Dr Sharad K. Soni, whose pioneering work on Mongolia inspired me, for his unconditional support in completion of this work. I take this opportunity also to thank my husband without whom my efforts would not have been fruitful and the love and care of my two sons who are always there to support me.

Last but not the least I place my sincere gratitude to all the staff members of Central Library of Jawaharlal Nehru University, Nehru Memorial Museum Library, Central Secretariat Library, and Institute for Defence and Strategic Analyses. I would place on record my thanks to Kalpaz Publication for publishing this book.

1

Introduction

Traditional balance-of-power theory, largely derived from the European experience, indicates that Mongolia is something of a power vacuum and that each of its powerful neighbours, China and Russia, remains tempted to fill that vacuum in order to prevent the other from doing so.[1] Today, as in the past, only Russia has the potential capability and interests necessary to protect Mongolia from Chinese and only China is in a position to afford Mongolia similar protection against Russia. That is how Mongolia's relations with its two neighbours can be described in spite of a comparatively close association with the Russians at least since 1921 when Mongolia became independent from the Chinese yoke. After Mongolia achieved statehood in 1924 and came to be known as the Mongolian People's Republic (MPR), its international relations were confined just to the diktat of the former Soviet Union until the latter's disintegration in 1991. It was due to the Soviet support and its recognition of Mongolia in 1924 that the whole period that followed witnessed Mongolia becoming one of the staunchest Soviet allies.

The background story of Mongolia-Russia relations demonstrates that for centuries, Mongolia was a territorial buffer. When the Manchus subjugated China and established the Qing empire in 1644, they also brought Mongolia under their dominion. But when the Qing empire collapsed in 1911, Moscow sucked Mongolia into its own expanding sphere of influence.[2] Early history of Russia-Mongolia relations suggests that the two sides came into contact as a result of "the steady Russian eastward movement across Siberia, which also involved settlements of Russians on the long common border between the two countries ... [and that] Russian activism in this area [Mongolia] began in the middle of the nineteenth century."[3] By then Mongolia had already become one of the key areas of the "Great Game" in the struggle for empire between Russia and China. While Russians usually regarded Mongolia as a buffer state, the Chinese viewed Mongolia as historically part of China. But the fall of the Manchu-Qing dynasty in 1911 cleared the way for Mongolia to assert for preserving its independence as a nation in the midst of the two hegemonic powers. Soon after Mongolia discarded its inclusion in the newly established Republic of China as Mongolians believed that Mongolia had just enjoyed a special relationship with the Qing court, and so it was not an integral part of China.

In sharp contrast, the Chinese maintained that Mongolia was an integral part of China, but they did not have the military strength to force the integration of Mongolia into Republic of China. Tsarist Russia did not recognise Mongolia's independence but it did provide Mongolia significant political, financial, and military support. Russian policy, at that time, was just to preserve Mongolian autonomy from China rather than supporting Mongolian independence in order to maintain Russia-China relations.[4] From 1911 to 1915, Russia, Mongolia, and China engaged in difficult negotiations, including frequent secret bilateral talks, and military posturing that eventually led to a tripartite agreement known as Kiakhta agreement concluded in June 1915.[5] The agreement came up with the broadest possible "autonomy" for Mongolia, then called Outer Mongolia.[6] However, following the 1917 Russian Revolution, China renewed its efforts to assert control over Mongolia and under pressure from Beijing,

Mongolia "petitioned" for abolition of its autonomy in November 1919. But this reassertion of Chinese control did not last long as Soviet Russia ultimately lent its support for Mongolian independence. China, on the contrary, persistently attempted to absorb Mongolia into the new Chinese nation-state.[7] In the meantime, Mongolia became a battleground in the Russian civil war and the White Russians drove the Chinese from Mongolia in 1921, thus paving the way for the establishment of the Mongolian People's Republic.

Since then the whole span of 20th century saw Mongolia being closely allied to that of the Soviet Union. The two sides remained very close so much so that even adoption of Communist ideology and policies were hardly distinguishable from the USSR. Mongolia found itself totally dependent on Soviet Union in all fronts – diplomatic, political, military and economic.[8] Many of Mongolia's cities, including the capital, Ulaanbaatar, resembled their Soviet counterparts,[9] and, during the period of Sino-Soviet antagonism from the mid-1960s to 1989, the Soviet troops and military equipment remained stationed in Mongolia to enhance its strategic advantage over China. For Moscow, Mongolia was then a territorial buffer due to its landlocked geographical location which forced Mongolia to serve as a shield behind which Russia felt more secure than if Mongolia had been in China's hands.[10] Naturally, taking due note of limitations imposed on its geographical setting, the extent and pattern of Mongolia's external relations has been influenced by and was heavily oriented towards Soviet Union.[11]

The whole relationship between Mongolia and Russia during the Soviet days can be described in terms of Soviet domination, particularly in Mongolia's domestic politics. Mongolia carried out the imitation of the Soviet policies to a great extent. Nearly all kinds of Soviet instruments, "both traditional Russian forms and new Communist ones, were coordinated to ensure that nobody other than the USSR would exercise any real control in the country." The ideological factor further made the Soviet task easy to play a role of "big brother" in Mongolia's domestic and foreign policies. In fact, spread of socialism in Mongolia took place through revolutionising influence of the October Revolution in Russia, the aid of the Comintern and Russian Communist (Bolshevik) Party, the upsurge of the Mongolian anti-colonial and anti-feudal struggle, growth of national and class consciousness, political leadership of the Mongolian People's Revolutionary Party (MPRP) and the establishment of the dictatorship of working *arats*.[12] All these processes finally led to the Sovietisation of the political activity in Mongolia. Already in late 1921, in return to the Soviet recognition of an independent Mongolia, the Mongolian government made a commitment to expedite social and economic changes in accordance with Soviet ideological mandates.[13] However, it was only in the 1940s that the Mongolian People's Republic became a "true Communist State."[14]

From the very beginning Soviet infiltration of Mongolia was carried on through three different channels: (1) by official representative of the Soviet government in Mongolia; (2) by representatives of the Comintern; and (3) by Buriat-Mongol citizens of the U.S.S.R. who had racial and religious affinity with the people of Mongolia and lived on the territory adjoining them.[15] However, Comintern's assistance to the MPRP also played a significant role in developing the latter into not only a mature Marxist-Leninist Party but also served as the major Soviet instrument for direct negotiations with the Mongols. The reshaping of Mongolian society from a traditional feudal society of pastoral nomads into a modern society of motorcycle-mounted shepherds and urban factory workers reflected both strong guidance and a high level of economic assistance from the Soviet Union.[16] The relations between Mongolia and the Soviet Union were so close that the ruling Mongolian People's Revolutionary Party faithfully echoed the line of the Communist Party of the Soviet Union (CPSU). In such a scenario, some Western observers even "doubted the reality of Mongolia's independence,"[17] while some described it as "the first Soviet satellite".[18]

Since both the domestic as well as foreign policy of Mongolia was controlled by the Soviet Union, it is found that the relationship between the two sides "was not based on equality and respect rather it was most unequal."[19] It was more so because the Soviet Union used various methods to consolidate its control in Mongolia. The Soviet-Mongol treaty relationship was, in reality, one of the devices used by the Soviets to fulfill their own objectives. The treaties and agreements included the Soviet-Mongolian Agreement of 1921 which constituted the basis of the international status of Outer Mongolia; Soviet-Mongol Gentlemen's Agreement of 1934 which provided for Mongolia's defence and mutual aid in case of attack by a third country;[20] and a ten-year Protocol of Mutual Assistance of 1936.[21] As a result, Soviet Union began looking upon Mongolia as a "protectorate", which turned out to be vital for Soviet Union's own strategic needs. By providing political, economic and military assistance to the Mongols, Soviets not only succeeded in dominating the MPR but also made it possible to have the Mongols militarily and morally on the USSR's side in the Second World War, particularly in the Far East.[22]

Remarkably, China's internal problems prevented it from reasserting its control over Mongolia; the most it could do was to protest the Soviet-Mongolian agreements concluded till the Yalta Conference took place.[23] It was indeed two decades later at the Yalta Conference in 1945 that the issue of Mongolian independence got a fillip when the Allied powers agreed that the *status quo* in Mongolia should be preserved after the Second World War.[24] Following a plebiscite in Mongolia that overwhelmingly supported independence, the Kuomintang government of China unwillingly agreed to recognise Mongolia's independence in 1946.[25] After the expiry of the Soviet-Mongol treaty of 1936, another treaty of Friendship and Mutual Assistance was signed in 1946 along with an agreement on Economic and Cultural Cooperation, which were followed by a number of other agreements especially in economic and trade fields. Mongolia was also the first Asian country to join the Council for Mutual Economic Assistance (CMEA) on 7th June 1962.[26] In fact, it was a device for integrating the economies of the socialist countries more closely with the economy of the Soviet Union.[27]

Mongolia-Soviet Union ties were further strengthened after signing of a twenty year new treaty of Friendship, Co-operation and Mutual Assistance in 1966 after the expiry of the treaty of 1946. This treaty created the basis for the Soviet military assistance to Mongolia. In accordance with this treaty, in 1967 the Soviet Union introduced its military units in Mongolia which could play a defensive as well as offensive role along its eastern flank. In the same year, a parade in Ulaanbaatar honored the fiftieth anniversary of the Bolshevik Revolution in 1917 and showed off new weapons, including Mongolian army-manned SA-2 surface-to-air and SNAPPER anti-tank guided missiles.[28] Since then China continued to demand the withdrawal of Soviet troops from Mongolia as a pre-condition for the normalisation of its relations with the USSR. On its part the Soviet Union was in no hurry to withdraw its troops from Mongolia as the former did not wish to create any security problem on the border which could also pave the way for its first satellite country in Asia to be away from Soviet influence. In 1989, the treaty of 1966 was extended automatically for a further period of ten years.

However, already in 1986, the period of tense Sino-Soviet and Sino-Mongolian relations seemed to be over as Soviet Union decided to withdraw its troops from Mongolia as part of Vladivostok initiative of the Soviet President Mikhail Gorbachev.[29] Mongolia, therefore, in modern times has been heavily influenced by China and Russia, the two countries between which it is geographically sandwiched. It achieved its independence only a few years after the Russian Revolution, adopted a socialist economic system modeled on the Soviet Union, and for nearly seven decades sought to impose its designs for a socialist state in practically every political, economic, and social dimension of life. In fact, policies of socialisation were applied to grazing–one of the most difficult activities to collectivise. Even the livestock raised by the nomadic population were placed under state ownership. As Asian members of COMECON (CMEA), Mongolia and Vietnam saw their economies integrated into Soviet/East European frameworks for the international division of labour.[30]

In the late 1980s, when it was evident that the Soviets and East Europeans had reached the brink of economic collapse, Mongolia's government decided to embark on a program of reforms aimed at breaking the country out of its own economic deadlock. However, Mongolia did not initiate any major moves toward political democratisation or free-market economic liberalisation until the early 1990s, after the Soviet Union had crumbled and the COMECON framework had been dismantled. Nonetheless, the historical pattern of its economic transition coincided with that of the Soviet Union and its East European allies, and its strategies and policies for the process closely resembled the "shock therapy" approach these countries employed.[31] Since 1990, Mongolia has been engaged in a process of institutional reform and policy transition that began with revisions to its constitution and that included legislative steps aimed at creating a parliamentary democracy and a market economy. The first stage of this process was put into effect by the coalition that won control of the government in the first round of general elections. That coalition was headed up by the Marxist Mongolian People's Revolutionary Party, the former communist party which eventually became a parliamentary democratic party.

In fact, modeled on the Soviet *perestroika* policy shift of the mid-1980s, political reforms in Mongolia began primarily as a drive to rebuild the economy.[32] Gradually, though, they began to assume a politicised dimension, and ultimately evolved into a full-fledged democratisation movement.[33] What really came out of the 1990 democratic revolution was that it "became a catalyst of new thinking in all spheres".[34] First of all it saw a profound change in Mongolia's political life. As a result of opposition demonstrations which started in December 1989, there had been major changes on the part of the MPRP. On 21st January 1990, the MPRP decided to end party privileges such as the closure of special shops, rest homes and hospitals, and a decrease in the number of official cars. At the 12-14 March 1990 plenum the members of the Politburo resigned and it was decided to end the 'leading and guiding role' of the party. A new General Secretary of the MPRP was elected and even a new President and a Prime Minister. The Politburo became known as the 'Presidium' and the General Secretary as 'Chairman', which was decided at the extraordinary party Congress held on 10-12 April 1990, the first since 1921. Presidium members were not allowed to hold state posts in order to separate party from state.[35] Further, Article 82 of the constitution was formally abolished on 23rd March 1990 as it described the MPRP as the 'guiding force' in society and the 'vanguard of the working people'. The extraordinary congress also ended party control over trade unions, cultural activities, the media, science and youth, although party cells were to remain in the police and army.

Independent parties were formally legalised at the 10-11 May 1990 session of the Great *Hural* (National Assembly). Free elections were held in July 1990 in which the MPRP competed against independent parties for the 430 seats in the Great *Hural*.[36] The MPRP had a successful election, winning 345 out of 430 seats in the Great *Hural* and over 60 per cent of the votes for the Little *Hural*. The turnout was 92.4 per cent showing great enthusiasm as the MPRP campaigned on a platform of 'humanitarian democratic socialism' and a 'state-controlled market economy' with more specific pledges including cancelling the debts of agricultural co-operatives. Other parties competing in the election included the Mongolian Democratic Party, the National Progress Party and the Social Democratic Party (these parties together forming an electoral alliance and outperforming the other opposition parties), the Free Labour Party, the Greens and the Patriotic Front. The Mongolian Democratic Party was in favour of a more market-orientated economy, while the Free Labour Party insisted on privately run shops and enterprises as well as market prices. Following elections a coalition government of three political parties ruled the country from 1990 to 1992, during which they took several important decisions towards democracy and market economy.[37]

In 1992, the MPRP won a majority in parliamentary elections and with that reinforced mandate, pushed ahead with the transition process. It all happened due to the end of an era of one-party rule by the MPRP, and unveiling a new constitution that abandoned socialism and changed the country's name from Mongolian People's Republic to simply "Mongolia". As a result, Mongolia's foreign relations posture shed its deep-seated dependence on the former Soviet Union and shifted toward a policy of non alignment shaped by balanced relations with Russia and China as well as with the US and other Western powers. The whole policies on foreign relations were shifted in conjunction with the structural transition. Some years prior to its breakup, the Soviet Union began withdrawing forces it had stationed in Mongolia, effectively bringing an end to a long-standing bilateral military alliance. From an international security standpoint, Mongolia has since pursued a policy aimed to balance its diplomatic ties with Russia, China, and Western powers, including the United States.[38] From a Northeast Asian security standpoint, Japan and the US welcomed this shift in foreign policy, especially in view of Mongolia's geopolitical significance as a vast territorial buffer between Russia and China. Needless to say, Mongolia required export markets as well as sources for imports of essential goods in order to make progress in developing its economy. That is why close economic ties with Russia and China have always been so vital.

However, throughout the 1990s, given the economic realities in Russia and China, Mongolia had little choice but to seek economic assistance not only from international organisations but also from Japan and other leading industrial powers in order to fulfill its efforts in structural transition. From 1980 to 1990, real GDP growth in Mongolia averaged a respectable 6.2 per cent per annum. With the start of the 1990s, however, the country entered a difficult new phase prompted by an external blow, i.e., the collapse of the Soviet Union. In structural terms, the Mongolian economy was heavily dependent on the former Soviet Union up to the end of the 1980s. As a country integrated into the old COMECON framework for the international division of labor, Mongolia carried out almost 95 per cent of all its foreign trade with the CMEA countries, of which over 80 per cent with the Soviet Union alone.[39] Mongolia exported copper and other mineral resources along with wool and leather products in return for imports of machinery, machine parts, and energy resources (the country was dependent entirely on the Soviet Union for oil imports). On top of this, injections of Soviet aid amounted to more than 40 per cent of Mongolia's net material product. In fact, practically all major engineered structures and other key components of infrastructure now operational in Mongolia were completed with the help of Soviet or East European aid. Even the new industrial center of Darkhan is widely recognised as an achievement backed by Soviet-led aid. Given this relationship of dependence, the Mongolian economy was effectively shaken to its very foundations once the Soviet Union finally crumbled.

Once having a distinction of being the second communist state of the world after the former Soviet Union, Mongolia's transition to a democratic state structure has not been an easy task, since it remained isolated from the outside world except the Soviet Union for almost seven decades.[40] During these intervening period, the extent and pattern of Mongolia's domestic and external politics was not only oriented towards Soviet Union but was even shaped under latter's influence.

In other words, the geopolitical situation prevailing in the region at that time provided the Soviet Union with an opportunity to steer the course of political, social, economic and strategic developments in Mongolia. But collapse of the Soviet Union in 1991 altered the whole scenario in Ulaanbaatar-Moscow relations, partly due to changes in the geopolitics of the region, which "has always played a decisive role in the history of Mongolia".[41] The post-Soviet transition in Mongolia also gave way to the beginning of a new era in the bilateral relations between Mongolia and Russia.

It is against this background that the next three chapters examine the course of post-1991 Mongolia-Russia re-engagement in different spheres, such as political, economic and strategic in the light of Mongolia being a de-Sovietised state and Russia no longer remaining a Soviet like Super power. However, one needs to have a look on the literature surveyed for this study so that a gap could be identified.

Survey of Literature

Mongolia-Russia relations have a unique historical, political and economic background which has been studied by various scholars. The literature available on this can also provide a better understanding of Mongolia's geostrategic importance so much so that it was reduced to a buffer status between its two immediate neighbours-Russia and China particularly in the second half of the twentieth century. And this status was altered only after the demise of the former Soviet Union, which gave way for Mongolia to open itself to the outside world by adopting an independent "multi-pillared" foreign policy. In the post-Cold War period Mongolia's relations with Russia has been witnessing a sea change from what it was during the Soviet days which came into light in various publications.

To begin with, an edited volume *Mongolia in the Twentieth Century: Landlocked Cosmopolitan* by Stephen Kotkin and Bruce Elleman (1999) examines Mongol history over the past century, embracing not only Mongolia proper but also Mongol communities in Russia and China. The contributions in this book are based on new archival research and the latest fieldwork dealing with Sino-Russian competition over Mongolia, international diplomacy in Mongolia as well as contemporary issues ranging from economic and cultural change to nationalism and emergent elites, apart from dealing with the post-Cold War Mongolian foreign policy and its implications for Mongolia's relations with Russia and China.

Ts. Batbayar and Sharad K. Soni's (2007) *Modern Mongolia: A Concise History* traces the history of the twentieth century Mongolia beginning from 1911 when the independence of theocratic Mongolia was proclaimed until the events leading to the June 2004 Parliamentary elections, with particular focus on Mongolia's ongoing foreign policy as well as revival of history, culture and religion which experienced a set back during the Soviet days. It also deals with the 1990 pro-democracy and national movement which resulted in the identity construction based on nomadism and Buddhism.

Christopher Kaplonski (2004) in his work *Truth, History and Politics in Mongolia: The Memory of Heroes* highlights the fact that since the middle of the twentieth century Mongolian history had been written as socialist history, and followed the dictates of Soviet historiography. He emphasised that in the writing and presentation of history, like politics more generally, Mongolia played the younger brother to the Soviet Union's elder brother, who provided guidance and direction.

Morris Rossabi's (2005), *Modern Mongolia: From Khans to Commissars to Capitalists* deals with the problems in Mongolia the reformers have had since the collapse of communism there. With the termination of crucial Russian economic support, free-market ideology advanced by the IMF, the World Bank and the ADB replaced the old commitment to central planning. Mongolia was pressured to go the "shock therapy" route, and the resulting transition was rougher even than Russia's, with inflation reached much higher than expected. However, he argues that the Mongolian reformers through their skillful efforts for democratisation brought their country into the international system.

Sharad K. Soni (2002) in his *Mongolia-Russia Relations: Kiakhta to Vladivostok* analyses not only the historical roots of Mongolia-Russia relations but examines in detail the extent and pattern of the whole gamut of their relations both during the Tsarist Russian as well as the Soviet period. Another work by Sharad K. Soni (2006) entitled *Mongolia-China Relations: Modern and Contemporary Times,* investigates the former Soviet Union's paramount role in Mongolia right from 1921 onwards, which affected the Sino-Mongolian relations keeping it subordinate to Sino-Soviet relations. But improvement in Mongolia-Russia co-operation after 2000, as he argues, raises concerns for China as it does not want Russia to regain its position of Soviet times in Mongolia.

While Kh. J. Bayasakh (2000) in his article "Mongolia and Russia-China in the New Millennium" *(China Report,* vol. 36, No.1) stresses that this post-Cold War trilateral relationship will continue in a positive direction unless there is a political breakdown in Russia or there is a radical change in PRC's policy towards Taiwan, Rajan Menon (2001), in his article "Russia," (in Richard J. Ellings and Aaron L. Friedberg, eds., Strategic Asia 2001–02), looks at contemporary Mongolia as a little importance to Russia. But Ts. Batbayar (2003) in his article "Mongolian-Russian Relations in the Past Decade" (Asian Survey, Vol. 43, No. 6) strongly disagrees. Because of its location between Russia and China, today, as in the past, Mongolia remains to be of strategic importance to Russia, and that the latter would use every opportunity to strengthen its position there.

William R. Heaton (1992) in his article "Mongolia in 1991: The Uneasy Transition" *(Asian Survey,* Vol. 32, No. 1) examines Mongolia's relationship with its neighbours which reflected its reversal of fortune because relations with the Soviet Union and constituent republics were troubled due to the sharp reduction in Soviet aid and the difficulties in securing supplies. After more than a decade Nyamosor Tuya (2005) in her article "Mongolia in 2004: Testing Politics and Economy" (Asian Survey, Vol. 45, No.1) deals with the state of Mongolia's domestic politics, economy as well as foreign affairs on the eve of not only 2004 Parliamentary elections but also the visit of Russian Foreign Minister Igor Ivanov to Mongolia and the latter acquiring an observer status of Shanghai Cooperation Organisation (SCO).

Importance of Mongolia in Asian security and assessment of external security environment have been assessed in various works. Donrov Ganbaatar (2001) in his Mongolia's Search for Security throws light on the new security environment of Mongolia and examines the dilemmas and opportunities facing Mongolia in the post-Cold War period following the demise of the Soviet Union and withdrawal of Soviet troops from its territory. Similarly, Sharad K. Soni (2006) in his article "Mongolia's Security Thinking and Outside World: A Reappraisal" *(Bimonthly Journal of Mongolian and Tibetan Current Situation,* Vol. 15, No. 6) argues that cooperation with the international community, active participation in regional and international arrangements, and creating a security regime in Northeast Asia comprise Mongolia's search for a 'third option', but at the same time he stresses that Mongolia sees maximum benefits through multilateralism. However, a latest work by Alicia Campi and Ragchaa Baasan (2009) entitled *The Impact of China and Russia on United States-Mongolian Political Relations in the Twentieth Century,* focusses more on large external powers, such as the US, Germany, or Japan, which could act as a "Third Neighbour" for Mongolia to counterbalance the traditional roles played by Mongolia's two border neighbours.

Another recent study carried out by Allan M. Wachman (2009) in his book *Mongolia's Geopolitical Gambit: Preserving a Precarious Independence While Resisting "Soft Colonialism"* highlights that Mongolia's independence has been affected by geopolitical rivalries among the great powers, particularly for access to Mongolia's mineral and energy resources, leaving Mongolia vulnerable to "soft colonialism," in which its economic and political autonomy may be compromised. Whereas J. Enkhsaikhan (2001) in his article "Mongolia's Status: The Case for a Unique Approach" *(Asian Affairs,* Vol. 27, No. 4) focuses on Mongolia's foreign policy initiatives to promote its security interests, primarily by political and legal means, P. Stobdan (1992) in his article "Mongolia in Strategic Vacuum" *(Strategic Analysis,* Vol.15, No. 2) and Eric A. Hyer (2005) in his article "Haunted by History: China and its North Western Neighbours" (Historica Actual Online, No.7) too deal with Mongolia's security dilemmas in the post-Cold War period.

The book *Mongolia: Tryst with Change and Development* edited by R.C. Sharma (1997) contains several articles on Mongolia's post-Cold War society, economy and trade, politics as well as its international relations. Another book entitled *Mongolia: Culture, Economy and Politics* edited by R.C. Sharma, K. Warikoo, Mansura Haider and Sh. Bira (1992) includes relevant articles on various issues confronting Mongolia following the break up of the former Soviet Union.

Since Mongolia is a landlocked country, a wider analysis of landlocked States in the world whose numbers have increased to over forty has been given in "Landlocked States of Africa and Asia" edited by Dick Hodder, Sarah J. Lloyd and Keith McLachlan (1998). Alan J.K. Sanders' "Mongolia: Looking to the Sea" talks not only about Mongolia's attempts to develop road and rail links with Russia for overcoming its landlocked position but also rebuilding relations with China in order to gain access to sea. Martin Ira Glassner in the same book provides a theoretical and background material on the problems of landlockedness and what can actually be done to resolve or at least mitigate these problems. Dick Hodder's final conclusion sums up the main issues arising in the context of landlocked states and offers tentative solutions. This is relevant in the Mongolian context as well which finds its expression in another publication entitled *Mongolian Futures: Scenarios for a Landlocked State* by Robert E. Bedeski (2008) which highlights the importance of external events, policy choices, and international supports for a landlocked State of Mongolia's future development and security, besides identifying economic reasons as key to the current development of Mongolia-Russia relations.

The literature surveyed above indicates that there are major limitations and gaps, which the current study seeks to fill. There has been no comprehensive work done on the re-engagement paradigm of Mongolia-Russia relations during the period of this study which has been undertaken. Whatever literatures are available they are generally confined to one or another aspect of relationship between Mongolia and Russia, and that too are short and limited articles mainly in informative forms which fail to analyse the significance of the entire gamut of relationship between the two countries. This study, therefore, is quite different in terms of dealing with the concerned issues thematically under different chapters, besides analyzing the trends within a broader perspective.

Notes and References

1. Alvin Magid and Richard W. Mansbach (1998), "Mongolian Security in the 21st Century: In Quest of Friends and Partners, not Allies", *The Mongolian Journal of International Affairs*, (5): 10-25
2. Allan M. Wachman (2009), *Mongolia's Geopolitical Gambit: Preserving a Precarious Independence while Resisting "Soft Colonialism"*, EAI Fellows Program Working Paper Series 18, Seoul: The East Asia Institute), p. 2.
3. Sharad K. Soni (2002), *Mongolia-Russia Relations: Kiakhta to Vladivostok*, Delhi: Shipra Publications and Maulana Abul Kalam Azad Institute of Asian Studies, p. 25.

4. Eric A Hyer. (2005), "Haunted by History: China and its Northwestern Neighbours", *Historia Actual Online,* (7): 83-92, URL: http://www.historia-actual.org/Publicaciones/index.php/haol/article/viewFile/ 102/93.
5. For details of 1915 Kiakhta Agreement on Mongolia's Status, see Sharad K. Soni (2006), *Mongolia-China Relations: Modern and Contemporary Times*, New Delhi: Pentagon Press, pp. 60-64.
6. Sharad K. Soni (2006), "India's New Role in East Asia: Implications for Mongolia," *The Mongolian Journal of international Affairs*, Ulaanbaatar, No.13, pp. 34-44.
7. T. Ewing (1980), *Between the Hammer and the Anvil? Chinese and Russian Policies in Outer Mongolia, 1911-1921*, Bloomington: Indiana University, Research Institute for Inner Asian Studies.
8. Soni (2002), *Mongolia-Russia Relations*, p. 7.
9. Foreign and Commonwealth Office, Government of the United Kingdom, Country Profile: Mongolia, 22 May 2009, at http://www.fco.gov.uk/en/travel-and-living-abroad/travel-advice-by-country/country-profile/asia-oceania/mongolia/?profile=intRelations
10. John Garver (1988), *Sino-Soviet Relations, 1937–1945: The Diplomacy of Chinese Nationalism*, Oxford: Oxford University Press, p. 217; Liu Xiaoyuan (2006), *Reins of Liberation: An Entangled History of Mongolian Independence, Chinese Territoriality, and Great Power Hegemony, 1911-1950*, Stanford: Stanford University Press, p. 342.
11. Soni (2002), *Mongolia-Russia Relations*, p. 85.
12. Alan J.K. Sanders (1987), *Mongolia: Politics, Economics and Society,* London: Frances Pinter, p. 26.
13. Serge M. Wolf (1929), "The People's Republic of Mongolia", *Contemporary Review* (London), March, p. 364.
14. Robert A. Rupen (1964), *Mongols of the Twentieth Century*, Bloomington: Indiana University, pt. I, p. 266.

15. Xenia Joukoff Eudin and Robert C. North (1957), *Soviet Russia and the East, 1920-1927: A Documentary Survey*, Stanford: Stanford University Press, p. 255.
16. Tripord, "Modern Mongolia", at http://aduuchin.tripod.com/mon/id18.html.
17. *Ibid.*
18. Eric A. Hyer (2005), "Haunted by History: China and its Northwestern Neighbours", *Historia Actual Online,* (7): 83-92, URL: http://www.historia-actual.org/Publicaciones/index.php/haol/article/viewFile/102/93.
19. Sharad K. Soni (2001), "Mongolia's Foreign Policy Priorities," *Himalayan and Central Asian Studies*, 5(1): 55-66.
20. This was a verbal agreement, see S. Avarzed (1958), "Foreign Policy of the Mongolian People's Republic", *International Affairs* (Moscow), 10: 39.
21. For the text of this treaty, see Leonard Shapiro, ed. (1955), *Soviet Treaty Series: A Collection of Bilateral Treaties, Agreements and Conventions etc. concluded between the Soviet Union and Foreign Powers, 1929-1939,* Washington. D.C.: The Georgetown University Press, Vol. 2, p. 162; New York Times, 8th April 1936.
22. Sharad K. Soni (2001), "Mongolia and the Soviet Union: A Study of Political Relations (1921-1990)," in Mahavir Singh, ed., Asia Annual 2001, Delhi: Shipra, p. 53.
23. Eric A. Hyer (2005), "Haunted by History: China and its Northwestern Neighbours", *Historia Actual Online,* (7): 87, URL: http://www.historia-actual.org/Publicaciones/index.php/haol/article/viewFile/102/93.
24. For details of Yalta diplomacy and the Mongolian Question, see Soni (2006):101-5.
25. Christopher P. Atwood (1999), "Sino-Soviet Diplomacy and Second Partition of Mongolia, 1945-46", in Stephen Kotkin and Bruce A. Elleman, eds., *Mongolia in the Twentieth Century: Landlocked Cosmopolitan*, Armonk, New York: M.E. Sharpe, , pp. 141-143.

26. Alois Holub (1980), "An Introduction to Problems of Economic Development in the CMEA Countries", *Global Economic Review*, 9 (2): 39.
27. For more on the Council for Mutual Economic Assistance (CMEA), also referred to as Comecon, see Lee Kendal Metcalf (1992),"Centripetal and Centrifugal Forces in the CMEA: Prospects for the Future", *Studies in Comparative Communism*, 25(2): 123-138.
28. GlobalSecurity.Org, "Group of Soviet Forces in Mongolia", at http://www.globalsecurity.org/military/world/russia/gsfm.htm
29. Sharad K. Soni (2006), *Mongolia-China Relations: Modern and Contemporary Times,* New Delhi: Pentagon Press, pp. 192-6.
30. Lee Kendal Metcalf (1992), "Centripetal and Centrifugal Forces in the CMEA: Prospects for the Future", *Studies In Comparative Communism*, 25(2): 127.
31. Morris Rossabi (2005), *Modern Mongolia: From Khans to Commissars to Capitalists,* Berkeley: University of California Press, p. 55.
32. Japan International Cooperation Agency (1997), *Country Study for Japan's Official Development Assistance to Mongolia*, Tokyo, p. 1.
33. *Ibid.*
34. Ts. Batbayar and Sharad K. Soni (2007), *Modern Mongolia: A Concise History,* New Delhi: Pentagon Press, p. 137.
35. Ian Jeffries (2007), *Mongolia: A Guide to Economic and Political Developments,* New York: Routledge, 1993: 126-7.
36. Sharad K. Soni (2004), "Democracy at Work: Parliamentary Elections in Mongolia," *Himalayan and Central Asian Studies*, 8(2-3): 105.
37. Baabar Batbayar (2001), "Post-Communist Transition in Mongolia", *Himalayan and Central Asian Studies,* 5(1): 55.

38. Bayarkuu, D. (2001), "Mongolia and its Third Neighbours", *Himalayan and Central Asian Studies,* 5(1): 84.
39. O. Nyamdavaa, (2001), "Mongolia-India Relations: Some Perspectives", *Himalayan and Central Asian Studies,* 5(1): 30.
40. Sharad K. Soni (2005), "Mongolia's Security Concerns in the Post-Cold War Period", in Mahavir Singh, ed., *Building a New Asia*, Delhi: Shipra, 283.
41. G. Tumurchuluun (2001), "Mongolia, Russia and China: The Geopolitical Perspective", *Himalayan and Central Asian Studies*, 5(1):33.

2

Political Relations

Relations between Mongolia and Russia have been traditionally strong, particularly since the Communist era, when Soviet Russia became the closest ally of the Mongolian People's Republic (MPR) and, therefore, in the western writings it was frequently referred to as a Soviet "satellite". But disintegration of the former Soviet Union in 1991 and consequently the collapse of the socialist system gave rise to a brand new external environment around Mongolia. Such a conducive environment was the result of the process of Soviet Style reforms and restructuring through *Iltod* and *Orchilan Baigalalt* which began in Mongolia in 1988. It provided good opportunity for both the Government and the people to carry out open discussions on the prevailing situation and find out ways to overcome the problem. The rapidity of change brought out in Mongolia was "largely due to the willingness and a welcoming acceptance of the democratic reforms urgently required for the prosperity of the Mongolian people not only in the domestic political, social and economic fields but also in the foreign affairs".[1] After the Soviet collapse, the geopolitical environment of Mongolia underwent a major change leaving the country in a "great power vacuum" but it proved to be profitable for Mongolia as it guided the country to achieve the following:[2] (a) For the first time in virtually seven decades, it provided an opportunity for Mongolia to open itself to the outside world and pursue an independent realistic multi-pillared foreign policy; (b) Non-aligned movement (NAM) admitted Mongolia as a full-fledged member which was not possible during the Soviet time due to the fear of likely impact on solidarity of the Socialistic bloc; and (c) Unlike in the past, Mongolia declared its attention of maintaining a balance in its relations with Russia and China, rather than giving importance to only one of them.

The emergence of new situation under the impact of political reforms and economic restructuring particularly during 1990-92, therefore, pushed Mongolia to think about its future development and security issues within the framework of new geopolitical realities. Mongolia's move towards democracy and a market economy necessitated a drastic shift in the strategies, purposes and priorities of its foreign policy. As such, Mongolia abandoned its "satellite state" foreign policy and developed an independent, non-aligned, multi-pillar and open foreign policy concept based on guidance by its national interests.[3] As a result, Mongolia's relations with Russia too underwent a change. Unlike Soviet period when dependence and domination were the two fundamental features characterising bilateral ties between the two sides, the post-1991 period witnessed quite a different pattern that was based on "equality" in relationship with the outside world including the two neighbours-Russia and China.

Mongolia's Foreign Policy Goals

The end of the Cold War provided an opportunity for various nations, particularly in Asia, to experience a complete change in the international order. In other words, as some analysts believe, "it was a return of history in diversity of new and emerging developments".[4] Another aspect of this changed scenario can be gauged from the fact that it gave enough space to nations to reanalyse the ideological and structural dimension of their policies in political, social, economic and cultural fields. This also meant recognising the contemporary changes and its sociological implications, making structural readjustment and reshaping the pattern of future growth and development in political-diplomatic spheres. Such changes have found their relevance in case of Mongolia as well. This is more so because the collapse of the erstwhile Soviet Union has also provided Mongolia a rare opportunity in its history to come out of Soviet grip and become part of the new international order. Significantly, the new emerging forces of globalisation led Mongolia to march ahead in search for a new national identity and recast her ties with the external world on a new basis. These processes were further accelerated by the democratic reforms "with stability based on peaceful evolution".[5] What is striking to note here is that unlike the Soviet period democratic reforms in Mongolia are now characterised by more flexible and pragmatic solutions to all the existing problems in all spheres of socio-economic and political domains. Moreover, these reforms paved the way for framing the governmental policies in such a manner that it could benefit Mongolia both internally and externally.[6] So far as external benefit is concerned Mongolia has been able to pursue the policy of maintaining cordial relations with rest of the countries, particularly in Asia.[7]

The first major change in terms of a new national identity took place on 28th November 1991 when Mongolia's State Great *Khural* (parliament) decided to change the name of the country from the Mongolian People's Republic to simply Mongolia, which was done in the new Constitution introduced on 12th February 1992.[8] The Constitution not only stressed on the adoption of political democracy and the market economy,[9] but also specified that "Mongolia shall adhere to the universally recognised norms and principles of international law and pursue a peaceful foreign policy". After its transformation into a democracy, Mongolia sought to establish a more-balanced relationship that placed it on equal terms with Russia. In 1994, the State Great *Khural* introduced a set of domestic and foreign policy guidelines that drove the country towards a new diplomatic course aimed at securing its own independence and sovereignty. The main objective was to balance its relations with Russia and China, and secondly, Mongolia was interested in promoting its ties with Japan, the US, Germany, and other leading industrial countries, and in fostering closer ties with countries of the Asia-Pacific region. Accordingly, it began pursuing an active multilateral diplomatic offensive because by then it was clearly understood by the Mongolian leaders that national security could only be ensured by securing international guarantees "through a combination of unilateral, bilateral and multilateral measures."[10] While economic development was one of the goals Mongolia had in mind with such strategies, gaining prestige for itself in the international community was also on the cards. By pursuing a diversified foreign policy, Mongolia was optimistic to work out on reassuring security arrangements in the new geopolitical environment.

The need for a new foreign policy was in fact felt back in 1986 when Gorbachev's Vladivostok initiative sought for withdrawal of Soviet troops from Mongolia. And later this was considered to be "a clear signal to Mongolia to examine a whole range of foreign policy options".[11] So, in 1989 it was realised that the principal motivation driving Mongolia's foreign policy was the preservation of territorial integrity, together with the projection of a substantial measure of political independence. As already mentioned, Mongolia often served as a Soviet proxy, representing the Soviet position when and where needed throughout the Cold War period. However, in the post-Cold War period Mongolia took a more balanced and pragmatic approach to the new global realities to which both domestic and international factors contributed tremendously. The key policy issues revolved around Mongolia included "national interest in the first place, depending upon how constructively the policy and strategy can achieve the defined goals".[12] Thus, the issue of national security which was actually "directly dependent on the international security" was taken as the most important factor while defining the goals of Mongolia's foreign relations. For that reason, the national security of Mongolia was divided into global, regional and sub-regional and Mongolian foreign policy has been framed accordingly. Finally, Mongolia came up with its "Multi-Pillared" foreign policy also known as "Multi-Dimensional" or "Omni-directional" foreign policy, the basic tenets of which were spelled out in the three inter-related documents, i.e., Concept of National Security, Concept of Foreign Policy and the Military Doctrine which were adopted by the State Great *Khural* in July 1994.[13]

The Foreign Policy Blue Book (2000) is another document which outlines Mongolia's foreign policy goals.[14] In fact, this multi-pillared foreign policy from the very early stage took a comprehensive account of traditional and non-traditional aspects of national security which helped in reshaping Mongolia's external relations on quite a new basis. The basic aim of Mongolia's foreign policy is to preserve the self-determination of the Mongol people[15] and to meet Mongolia's national interests, which are "the existence of the Mongolian people and their civilisation ... the country's independence, sovereignty territorial integrity ... relative economic independence, sustainable ecological development and national unity." (Concept of National Security, Point 3).[16] Of these the two most important are retaining sovereignty and economic independence.[17] In addition, Mongolia also pursues a policy of non-intervention in its neighbours' affairs, unless its own interests are jeopardised (Concept of Foreign Policy, Point 9).[18] As such, Mongolia's foreign policy is being guided by the following directions:[19]

(a) Maintaining friendly relations with the Russian Federation, People's Republic of China shall be priority directions of Mongolia's foreign policy activity. It shall not adopt the line of either country but shall maintain in principle a balanced relationship with both of them and shall promote all-round neighborly cooperation. In doing so, the traditional relations as well as the specific natures of our economic cooperation will these two countries will be taken into account.

(b) The second direction of Mongolia's foreign policy activity shall be developing friendly relations with highly developed countries of the West and East such as the United States of America, Japan and the Federal Republic of Germany. At the same time it will also pursue a policy aimed at promoting friendly relations with such countries as India, the Republic of Korea, Thailand, Singapore, Turkey, Denmark, the Netherlands, Finland, Austria, Sweden, Switzerland and at creating and bringing to an appropriate level their economic and other interests in Mongolia.

(c) The third direction of Mongolia's foreign policy activity shall be strengthening its position in Asia and securing a constructive participation in the political and economic integration process in the region. Within the framework of this objective, greater attention shall be given to Asia and the Pacific region, in particular to North-East and Central Asia. Mongolia shall take an active part in the process of initiating dialogues and negotiations on the issues of strengthening regional security and creating a collective security mechanism. It will strive to become a member of the Asia, Pacific Economic Co-operation (APEC) forum. Prerequisites for participating in regional integration shall be created primarily through expanding and promoting bilateral relations with the countries of the region.

(d) The fourth direction of Mongolia's foreign policy, activity shall be promoting cooperation with the United Nations Organisation and its specialised agencies, and with international financial and economic organisations, including the International Monetary Fund, the World Bank and the Asian Development Bank.

(e) The fifth direction of Mongolia's foreign policy activity will be developing friendly relations with countries of the former socialist community, as well as the newly independent states. When developing relations with these countries, a flexible approach will be adopted, reinforcing the positive legacy of our past relations while at the same time taking into account the potential of promoting relations in conformity with the new circumstances. Particular attention will be given to promoting relations with Poland, Hungary and the Czech Republic in Eastern Europe as well as with Kazakhstan, the Ukraine, Belarus, Kyrgyzstan and Uzbekistan.

(f) The sixth direction of Mongolia's foreign policy activity shall be developing friendly relations with developing countries and cooperating with them, as much as possible, in the solution of common objectives. Beyond the framework of bilateral relations with these countries, this task will be realised mainly through cooperation within the framework of international organisations and movements, such as the United Nations, the Group of 77 and the Non-Aligned Movement.

Notwithstanding the clear guiding principles of Mongolia's foreign policy, the concept of foreign policy puts emphasis on "equidistance" in maintaining relations with Russia and China, principally due to the historical, geographical and economic factors. The policy core is not to adopt the line of either of these two countries but maintain a balanced relationship with both of them. "It specifically underlined", as Oyun Sanjaasuren, the Minister for Foreign Affairs of Mongolia, pointed out while delivering a lecture at the Marshall Centre, Bavaria, Germany on 8th February 2008, that "a policy of non-involvement and neutrality would be pursued with regard to the disputes that could arise between the two neighbours, unless the latter directly, affected Mongolia's national interests, in which case it would follow its vital interests."[20] Whereas Mongolia now maintains a strategic partnership with Russia and partnership of good neighbourly friendship and cooperation with China, the so-called "third neighbour" policy also forms the part of its multi-pillar foreign policy, "which articulates a policy of balance."[21] In simple words, the "third neighbour" policy means that Mongolia will no longer be dependent only on one neighbour but rather on as many as countries and international institutions as possible. Evidently, during the period of democratic reforms especially in the mid-1990s when no single nation came forward to be understood in real terms as Mongolia's "third neighbour", Ulaanbaatar's thinking took a definite turn to forge a new relationship with North East Asia that went beyond economic ties to include political concerns.[22] As such, Mongolia tried to forge its relations with a whole community of developed countries in the East and West, including first and foremost the United States, international organisations and other stakeholders which could support its democratic nation building and development.

Post-1991 Scenario in Political-Diplomatic Relations

In accordance with its foreign policy concept, Mongolia's political-diplomatic relations with Russia during the period of this study began to take shape first and foremost through exchange of high level visits between the two sides. However, these visits did not yield the much desired results as one can witness a clear state of stagnation in their relations until the year 2000 when Russian President Vladimir Putin paid a visit to Mongolia. The reasons for their not so encouraging ties involve two key factors: (a) Dissolution of the former Soviet Union and the subsequent creation of Russian Federation, and (b) Change of Mongolia's official title in 1992 which symbolised the end of socialist ideologies. (Zhao 2005: 6). It was especially important for Mongolia to keep clinging to Russia. Yet this necessity was affected to a large extent by the "political ideology factor." It was more so because the main principles of socialist theory had played major roles in ideological repression of the Mongolian people.[23] For example, several political groups in Mongolia tried to remain rigid in their approach in order to avoid close contacts with Russia at least until 1996. The Mongolian Social Democratic Party (MSDP) and its Chairman B. Batbayar, in particular, adopted a cautious approach towards Russia. He considered the relationship between Mongolia and Russia as being "unequal" since the Soviet days, and, therefore, his argument was that "it would be in the best interests of Mongolia to strengthen ties with the West and Japan". [24]

On the other side, Russian policy towards Mongolia depended much on the extent of Russia's presence and influence in Asia which indeed saw a general decline in the early 1990s. Earlier, during the Cold War period the four major goals of Soviet policy in Asia were defence of the Soviet Union's eastern borders, including areas disputed with China, Japan, and Mongolia; maintenance of a set of alliances with key nations along the Asian periphery; improved relations with Western-oriented, relatively advanced states in order to obtain assistance in developing Siberia; and as much isolation as possible of China, South Korea, and the United States.[25] In order to fulfill these goals, the main instrument was the large Soviet military presence in Asia, which backed foreign policy assertions that the Soviet Union was an Asian power. But in the post-Soviet period, according to the 1993 draft foreign policy concept, Russia aimed to correct the imbalance in the former Soviet Union's East-West relations by paying greater attention to its ties with Asian states.[26] This observation "reflected the debate in Russian foreign policy between the westward-looking so-called Atlanticists and the so-called Eurasianists who would focus on relations with the near abroad and the wealthiest Asian states." Reflecting the Eurasian alternative, the 1993 draft foreign policy concept stressed on the need for a flexible policy of mutually beneficial relations with all the countries of Asia, thus fostering good relations by reducing Russian military forces and cooperating with the United States and other regional powers to bolster security and regional stability.[27] Such cooperation primarily included joint prevention of undesirable and unstable behavior, including organised crime and drug trafficking, and that by following such a policy, Russia came to be seen as an "honest prospective partner" in the whole region.

However, at the same time it has also been argued that

the Soviet collapse pushed Russia geopolitically towards Asia because a sizeable part of Russia's territory and resources is in its eastern regions. Moreover, the Russian territory directly touches three Asian states, i.e., China, Japan, and North Korea. Besides, the security of the large populations of Russians remaining in Central Asia, which has an extensive border with China, continued to be a major concern, and so events such as growing China-Kazakhstan relations provided added Russian attention on Asia.[28] As regards Russia's relations with Mongolia, there are evidences that their relationship has been affected not only by the developments taking place in Mongolia internally and externally but also due to separatism in areas of Russia bordering Mongolia. The break down in bilateral relations began to be felt in the beginning of the 1990s itself despite the visit of the Mongolian Prime Minister D. Byambasuren to Moscow in February 1991, during which the two sides concluded a new Declaration on Friendship and Good-Neighborly Cooperation including a protocol on economic cooperation. But it did not bring the required results and instead went towards stagnation in the overall relationship between the two countries due to the following down turn initiatives: Firstly, Soviet-era construction projects were quickly withdrawn; secondly, trading of Mongolian copper and other minerals, meat products, leather goods, and carpets for Russian oil and energy-related spare parts in a new hard currency system had to be suspended because Moscow had no funds; and lastly, the issue of the huge Mongolian debt to Russia could not be resolved.[29]

Nevertheless, Mongolia began taking serious steps towards restoration of its relations with Russia at all levels. The Mongolian President's visit to Moscow in January 1993 was a major event, which included the signing of a new twenty-year Treaty on Friendly Relations and Co-operation between the two countries as well as a Joint Statement condemning mass reprisals during the 1930s-1940s in the former Soviet Union and Mongolia. The Treaty on Friendly

Relations and Cooperation was signed on 20th January 1993 by the then Russian President Boris Yeltsin and Mongolian President P. Ochirbat, the first President of Mongolia, which "marked not only the beginning of changes in Russia-Mongolia relations but also a rethinking by the two sides of their foreign policy doctrine and the liberalisation of their multilateral and bilateral relations".[30] This new Treaty, which replaced the Treaty of Friendship, Cooperation and Mutual Assistance concluded between the former Soviet Union and the Mongolian People's Republic on 15th January 1966[31] required that both sides respect each other's status as sovereign and independent nations and not to resort to the use of force to invade each other's territory, not to interfere with each other's internal affairs, and show mutual respect for human rights and fundamental freedom.

Russia and Mongolia, reads Article 1 of the Treaty, "consider themselves as friendly nations and their relationship will be guided by the principle of respect for each other's state sovereignty and independence, of being equally sovereign, of non-use of force, of not threatening with force, of inviolability of state frontiers, of territorial integrity, of non-interference in internal affairs; respect for fundamental human rights and liberties, for equality of rights, for the right to decide destiny on their own; and by the principle of fulfilling in good faith their obligations and cooperating as good neighbours and partners."[32]

Further, the reciprocal visits of high level officials in each other's countries continued for bilateral discussions on many issues. Yet both sides took cautious approach in implementing the measures towards forging a strong relationship, especially in the political field. For example, in April 1995, Mongolian Prime Minister P. Jasrai visited Moscow to negotiate with the then Russian Prime Minister V. S. Chernomyrdin.[33] Though the visit was marked by the signing of nearly a dozen agreements including those that dealt with scientific and cultural co-operation, cross-border travel by citizens of the two countries, cooperation in the areas of posts and communications, and trade and economic relations for the year 1995, nothing concrete could be noticed in their practical implementation. Still the issue of repayment of Mongolian debt to Russia continued to be a stumbling block in their relationship, which is evident from the fact that "during the Russian Foreign Minister Yevgeny Primakov's visit to Mongolia in November 1996, the two sides failed to resolve the issue [of debt repayment]".[34] Another problem that Mongolia and Russia struggled to resolve was related to law and order along their common borders, particularly along Mongolia's northwestern frontier of Tuva.[35] Criminal activities along the border such as smuggling of drugs, consumer goods and weapons for sale across Mongolian territory made the situation even worse. Later, a joint Russian-Mongolian border commission was formed in order to halt such incidents, it faced problems in continuing its activities due to lack of "necessary financial resources"[36]

Mongolia-Russia political-diplomatic relations experienced an improvement in 1999 largely due to the China factor as Chinese domination in Mongolian economy was clearly visible. Moscow began to realise the geopolitical importance of Mongolia in the light of Chinese presence which also raised Russian concerns for the security of its eastern borders. By then situation in Mongolia too became conducive for strengthening the ties with Russia. Already in a survey conducted in 1996, 79 per cent of the Mongolian public opinion went in favour of closer ties with Russia as against only 35 per cent in support of China.[37] In 1999, not only the 60th anniversary of the battle at the Khalkhin Gol River was celebrated in Mongolia, but also the meetings of veteran of both countries were held, and memorials were renovated. Reciprocal visits of the leaders of the State Great *Khural* and the State *Duma* took place, apart from organising the exchange of delegations from the two countries' security councils. Besides, the Foreign Ministry consultations were put into practice, including contacts at the ministerial level.

While in February 1999, Russian Foreign Minister Igor Ivanov visited Ulaanbaatar, in late 1999, his counterpart, N. Tuya paid a visit to Moscow. As a result, local regions of Mongolia and the Russian Federation that faced each other across the border started to build up direct ties. For example, the President of Russia's Siberian Republic of Buryatia and various regional governors visited Ulaanbaatar in 1999 to sign agreements on economic relations and cross-border contacts.[38] A long-awaited meeting between Russian President Boris Yeltsin and Mongolian President N. Bagabandi took place in Kremlin in December 1999 to discuss several important issues of mutual concerns in almost all areas-political, economic, cultural and military.[39] Encouraging signs also emerged on the thorny issue of Mongolia's debt repayment when the two leaders agreed to advance the continuing negotiations on the matter. Thus, "delinking from Russia" that was applied to the newly independent Central Asian States[40] seems to have been a reality in Mongolia throughout the 1990s until the issuance of the Ulaanbaatar Declaration in 2000 which injected new energy into the relationship between the two countries.

Ulaanbaatar Declaration: Beginning of a New Era

Though Russia's interaction with Mongolia remained limited during the period from 1991 to 1999, it witnessed the beginning of a new era since the year 2000. Earlier, Russia did not have to "share" Mongolia with other powers during the years when the Soviet Union existed.[41] But the post-Soviet period saw both the Chinese as well as Americans apart from others roaming the corridors of Mongolian bastions of power seeking deals, offering investments, and exercising clout. This situation alarmed the Russians to have its benign presence in Mongolia before it becomes too late, which ultimately resulted in the signing of the Ulaanbaatar Declaration while the Russian President Vladimir Putin was visiting Mongolia on November 13-14, 2000. Putin's visit to Mongolia was captioned by a Russian newspaper, *Nezavisimaya Gazeta* [Independent Newspaper] dated November 15, 2000, as “Kremlin Brought Back to Mongolia: Vladimir Putin Agrees to Resume Bilateral Relations to Full Extent”. [42] It was indeed a significant event for both the countries as the last visit by a Russian President had taken place 26 years ago, i.e., in 1974 when Leonid Brezhnev undertook a journey to Mongolia. Both sides had high hopes that Putin would be able to revive Russia-Mongolia relations to their full strength and he too did not waste time but gave statement like the two countries' bilateral relations required “intensification.”

What came into fore was that the two sides signed a 25-point memorandum of cooperation termed as “Ulaanbaatar Declaration” on November 14, 2000. It was a document which determined the principles of directions of extending and developing Mongolia-Russia relations in the 21st century. The declaration displayed that “in many cases both countries see eye to eye on the most important aspects of the global situation, and sets forth the willingness of Moscow and Ulaanbaatar to closely coordinate their policy in international affairs on a wide range of issues”.[43] The leaders of the two countries held a thorough exchange of views on a broad range of questions concerning their bilateral relations and on international issues of mutual interest, which constitute an important stage in the development of the traditional friendly relations between them. The two sides also agreed to intensify negotiations on bilateral issues and to bring them to a conclusion by the end of 2001. So far as the political relations are concerned, the Ulaanbaatar Declaration reaffirmed the commitment to the Treaty of Friendship and Co-operation between Mongolia and the Russian Federation concluded on January 20, 1993. The two sides also made commitments that,

> Mongolian-Russian co-operation in various areas in the new century must move forward in accordance with the provisions of the Charter of the United Nations and the

> norms of international law and equity, the principles of respect for sovereignty, equality of rights, mutual advantage and territorial integrity, and also on the basis of the traditions of friendship and good-neighbourliness built up over many decades.[44]

Besides, as mentioned in the Ulaanbaatar Declaration, Mongolia and Russia came to an understanding that there was a "need to build a multipolar structure for peace, and [hence] underscored the special importance of the development of inter-State relations in Asia, without division into blocs." On the basis of this understanding both sides reaffirmed that "they will not participate in any military-political unions directed against each other, and undertake not to conclude with third countries any treaties or agreements which are incompatible with the interests of the sovereignty and independence of the other party." It was decided that "neither party will allow its territory to be used by a third State for the purposes of aggression or any other act of force prejudicial to the sovereignty, security and public order of the other party." Overall, Putin's visit to Ulaanbaatar aimed at improving the bilateral relations which had been facing stagnation for almost a decade. In fact, the credit for improvement in relations was also given to the overwhelming victory of the Mongolian People's Republican Party (MPRP) by defeating the Democrats in the June 2000 parliamentary elections. It was also an indication that "the Mongolian people reposed faith in the reformed MPRP, the former communists".[45] On the other side, Moscow regarded the MPRP government as more credible and more intent on improving bilateral relations. As such Putin's visit, combined with the MPRP victory, rekindled the hope for Russia and Mongolia to resume and promote their traditional ties. This, in the following years, ultimately gave a strong push to their so called halted relations and marked the return of Russia's comprehensive cooperation with Mongolia.

Since then the two sides witnessed several high level bilateral visits including the 2003 visit of Russian Prime

Minister Mikhail Kasyanov who became the first head of cabinet to come to Mongolia since 1971. Even the visits by Russian governors to different regions along the Mongolian border became more frequent. However, some scholars are of the opinion that since the signing of the Ulaanbaatar Declaration Putin's policy for Mongolia had been only moderately successful.[46] In particular the Economic constraints on the Russian side, combined with the troubled legacy of Soviet-Mongolian relations, proved to be a stumbling block in the full reconciliation of Mongolia-Russia relations. Other factors include concerns from both sides on the state of their relations with the outside world, mainly in the Asia-Pacific region. While Mongolia pursued its policy of maintaining "equidistance" with its two neighbours, Russia on its part continued its efforts to strike a balance in its relations with China and other powers in East Asia in order to counter growing US influence in the region. Nevertheless, it may be pointed out that Mongolia's greatest importance to Russia lies in its geopolitical location[47] and hence it was in the interest of Moscow to renew its relations with Mongolia. In that sense, Ulaanbaatar Declaration indeed saw not only the beginning of a new era in the relationship between the two countries but also helped Russia to try to reestablish its "preeminent position as most favoured neighbour."[48]

Commonality of Interests on Regional and Global Issues

While making efforts for ensuring security to its borders as well as having "stable" relations with immediate and distant neighbours.[49] Mongolia also placed a priority focus on regional and global issues, particularly those concerning the Asia-Pacific region. On such issues, there has been convergence of views between Mongolia and Russia, especially since the year 2000 when the two sides made several commitments. Mongolia's new diplomacy of nonalignment may be termed as a success because unlike the Soviet period, in the post-Soviet period it was welcomed by Russia. Moreover, in view of its geographic location, Mongolia has developed good relations not only with the neighboring countries of Russia and China but also with other regional and global powers. This was consistent with the approach set out in the Mongolia's Foreign policy concept, where strengthening of bilateral relations are seen as the building blocks for effective regional and global strategies.[50] Besides, over the past two decades, there has also been a cooperative relationship between Mongolia's foreign affairs and development:[51] Since Mongolia has established partnerships with neighbonring countries and many other countries around the world through open, peaceful and multi-faceted diplomacy, these partners have cooperated in Mongolia's development as well.

So far as Mongolia-Russia common interests on regional and global issues are concerned, initially the two sides did not demonstrate much eagerness due to factors already discussed in preceding paragraphs. But once the Ulaanbaatar Declaration was signed both sides began showing encouraging results. It was in fact the Russian Foreign Ministry which wanted to incorporate as many international issues as possible in the Ulaanbaatar Declaration in order to display the two countries' common interests on regional and global issues. As such Russia recognised Mongolia as a "factor of stability in Central Asia" and in return obtained commitments from Mongolia on such global issues as the "unique and universal role of the United Nations in the international system," "the need to preserve the missile defense treaty of 1972 as the cornerstone of strategic stability," and "participation of Mongolia in one or another way in the activities of the Shanghai Five regional grouping".[52] As regards the Shanghai Forum as an organisation, while the Russian side informed Mongolia about its aims, tasks and activities for the broad-based international cooperation, the Mongolian side quickly expressed its desire "of becoming involved in its work in some form."[53] Besides, the two sides not only welcomed "the development of regional and border contacts" but also promised "to make efforts to develop the legal basis for further expanding and deepening them." In particular, Mongolia had shown interests in "active cooperation with the regional structures of the Russian Federation, including the interregional association-Siberian Accord."

As proclaimed in the Ulaanbaatar Declaration, Mongolia and Russia made commitments "to closely coordinate their efforts on questions of peace, security and cooperation in the Asia-Pacific region." They took a positive view of the role of the Asean Regional Forum (ARF) and expressed their intention to make a worthwhile contribution to its work. It is to be noted that since joining the Asean Regional Forum in 1998, Mongolia has been taking an active participation in the Forum's activities, apart from seeking to become a member of the APEC and ASEM. Russia supports Mongolia's aspiration to become a member of the Asia-Pacific Economic Cooperation (APEC).[54]

As Mongolia wanted to contribute to the Asia-Pacific Multilateral Security Dialogue Mechanism,[55] in the Ulaanbaatar Declaration both sides expressed their full support for the official and informal structures for such dialogue for addressing current problems of regional security and cooperation. In addition, the two countries also expressed their support for increased dialogue through all channels with a view to establish an inter-State mechanism for security and cooperation questions especially in North-East Asia (NEA). It was more so because the North East Asian region has been considered as a major component of the broader Asia-Pacific economic structure and a pivot of the world power equation with the increasing interaction of China, Japan, Russia and the United States.[56]

More importantly, Mongolia accords special significance to North East Asia and Central Asia largely due to the fact that in the post-Soviet period it identifies itself more as a North East Asian country.[57] However, in October 2007 while addressing the scholars at the Center for Strategic and

International Studies in Washington DC, USA, the then Mongolian President Nambaryn Enkhbayar emphasised that Mongolia "belongs to both regions despite the fact that North East Asia and Central Asia are two very different regions in many respects".[58] But it is a matter of debate which has been continuing ever since Mongolia launched its new post-Soviet foreign policy concept. Coming back to common interests between Mongolia and Russia on regional and global issues, the Ulaanbaatar Declaration demonstrated that the two countries also welcomed "the outcome of the inter-Korean summit meeting held in Pyongyang from 13th to 15th June 2000" and hoped that "the process of reconciliation and cooperation on the Korean peninsula will develop further." They were convinced that "the maintenance of peace and stability on the Korean peninsula is a major precondition for stability in North East Asia and in the Asia-Pacific region as a whole." In such a situation, they made commitments to oppose "any unilateral or multilateral actions that might give rise to mutual mistrust between States in that part of the world."

Since both Mongolia and Russia have been increasingly active members of the regional and international community, they have distinction of also being supporters of the Global War on Terror. However, unlike Mongolia Russia has experienced the black spots of terrorism, particularly in Chechnya. As such both parties of the Ulaanbaatar Declaration decided to "join forces to oppose international terrorism, religious extremism and national separatism, which threaten regional security, stability and development, and also such forms of criminal activity as illicit trafficking in arms and narcotics and illegal migration." Commonality of interests between the two countries contributed much to the development of bilateral relations, especially since 2000. Mongolia, on its part, began the year 2001 with a strong emphasis on its course of rapprochement with the countries of the Asia-Pacific region as the then President Bagabandi visited South Korea, Singapore, India and Nepal, while

Prime Minister Enkhbayar went to Japan in February 2001 on his first official visit abroad since assuming office in July 2000. The consultations showed the growing interest of the parties concerned in holding talks not only on issues related to bilateral relations but also on broader regional security issues thus contributing to building of trust among countries. Earlier, President Bagabandi's participation in the UN Millennium Summit in 2000, was a strong indication of Mongolia's commitment to the ideals of the UN. Remarkably, Mongolia also is the world's first UN-recognised single-State Nuclear Weapon Free Zone which has been making a specific contribution to strengthening the regional peace and stability.

To conclude, the emergence of new situation under the impact of political reforms and economic restructuring as well as due to soviet collapse set Mongolia in motion to think about its future development and security issues within the framework of new geopolitical realities. This resulted in adopting a new "multi-pillar" foreign policy which broadened Mongolia's diplomatic outlook and the scope of its international activities, besides assuming a neutral posture in its relations with the two immediate neighbours-Russia and China. However, so far as its political relations with Russia are concerned, almost the whole period of 1990s saw stagnation despite the signing of 1993 treaty of friendly relations and cooperation as well as exchange of occasional high level bilateral visits. In mid-1990s some scholars argued in favour of Russian interest in having not only "a friendly Mongolia but also a Mongolia strategically allied with Russia".[59] Their contention was that "if Mongolia were to be dominated by China or any other nation, it would represent a dramatic shift in the balance-of-power in the entire region of the Asia and Pacific". Such thinking helped build up confidence on both sides to develop their relations. But the turning point came only in 2000 when Putin paid a visit to Mongolia, resulting in the signing of the Ulaanbaatar Declaration. Since then there is no looking back and moreover commonality of interests particularly on regional and global issues brought the relationship of the two countries in the political field to a new height. Unlike the Soviet period, when the determining aspect of Mongolia-Russia relations was ideology, in the post-1991 period it has been the mutual interest which formed the basis of close co-operation in all areas-political, economic and strategic.

Notes and References

1. Sharad K. Soni (2002), *Mongolia-Russia Relations: Kiakhta to Vladivostok*, Delhi: Shipra Publications, p. 222.
2. G. Tumurchuluun (1995), "Mongolia's Foreign Policy Revisited: Its relations with Russia and China in the 1990's", *The Mongolian Journal of International Affairs* (Ulaanbaatar), (2): 48-49.
3. See Mongoliana (2006), "Foreign Policy and International Relations," 4th January, URL: http://www.ub-mongolia.mn/facts-mongolia/political-system.html
4. D. Banerjee, (1992), "Neither War Nor Peace", *World Focus*, 13 (11-12): 11.
5. D. Bayarkhuu, (2003), "Post-Communist Transition and Common Ground: A Mongolian Perspective", *The Mongolian Journal of International Affairs* (Ulaanbaatar) (10): 67.
6. Sharad K. Soni (2003), *Mongolia between Russia and China: Emerging Equation*, Kolkata: Maulana Abdul Kalam Azad Institute of Asian Studies, p. 64.
7. J. Enkhsaikhan, (2000b) "Single State NWFZ: From Concept to Practice", *The Mongolian Journal of Strategic Studies*, (2): 19.
8. Mongolia and Tibetan Foundation (1992), The Constitution of Mongolia, Taipei,pp 1-31.
9. Ian Jeffries (2007), *Mongolia: A Guide to Economic and Political Developments*, New York: Routledge, p. 127.
10. Government of Mongolia (1998), Mongolian Defence White Paper, 1997-1998, Ministry of Defence, Ulaanbaatar, p. 29.
11. Alan J.K. Sanders (1987), Mongolia: Politics, Economics and Society, London: Frances Pinter, 1987, p. 26.
12. Sharad K. Soni (2008), "Post-Cold War Identity of Mongolia: Strategic Concerns", in P.L. Dash (ed.), *Emerging Asia in Focus: Issues and Problems*, Delhi: Academic Excellence, p. 420.

13. Sharad K. Soni (2001), "Mongolia's Foreign Policy Priorities," Himalayan and Central Asian Studies, 5(1): 55-66.
14. Government of Mongolia (2000), Mongolian Foreign Policy Blue Book, Ministry of External Relations, Ulaanbaatar.
15. Alicia J. Campi (1999), "Moving Mongolian Nomadism into the 21st Century: Cultural and Ecological Preservation Coupled with Economic Vitality and National Security", *Mongolica* (Ulaanbaatar), 9 (30): 550.
16. For the full text of Mongolia's National Security Document, see "Concept of National Security of Mongolia," *Mongolian Journal of International Affairs* (Ulaanbaatar), (2), 1995: 79-104.
17. Sarah Telford (2006), "To What Extent Does Post-1990 Mongolia Pursue an Independent Foreign Policy?", *Bimonthly Journal of Mongolian and Tibetan Current Situation* (Taipei, Taiwan), 15 (3), May: 56.
18. For the full text of Mongolia's Foreign Policy Document, see "Concept of Mongolia's Foreign Policy," *Mongolian Journal of International Affairs* (Ulaanbaatar), (2), 1995: 70-78.
19. Ts. Batbayar and Soni, Sharad K. (2007), *Modern Mongolia: A Concise History,* New Delhi: Pentagon Press. 121-123.
20. See Oyun Sanjaasuren (2008), "Mongolia's Foreign and Security Policy at the down of the New Century", Lecture, The Institute of Strategic Studies of the National Security Council of Mongolia, *The Mongolian Journal of Strategic Studies* , Ulaanbaatar, (2), 8th February: 13.
21. Allan M. Wachman (2009), *Mongolia's Geopolitical Gambit: Preserving a Precarious Independence While Resisting "Soft Colonialism",* EAI Fellows Program Working Paper Series 18, Seoul: The East Asia Institute.
22. Alicia Campi (2005), "Mongolia in Northeast Asiam-The New Realties", *The Wongolian Journal of International Affairs (*Ulaanbaatar), (12): 46-64. 51
23. D. Dashpurev and S.K. Soni (1992), *Reign of Terror in Mongolia*, New Delhi: South Asian Publishers. p.80.

24. Zhu-cheng Zhao (2005), "Mongolian Economic Security Policies toward Russia, 1990- 2000", *Bimonthly Journal of Mongolian and Tibetan Current Situation* (Taipei, Taiwan), 14 (2), March: 7.
25. Glenn E. Curtis, ed. (1996), *Russia: A Country Study*, Washington: GPO for the Library of Congress, URL: http://countrystudies.us/russia/86.htm,.
26. *Ibid.*
27. *Ibid.*
28. *Ibid.*
29. Alicia Campi (2004), "Mongolia in Northeast Asia — The New Realities," Taipei, Taiwan, September, URL: http://usmongoliagroup.com/article_northeastasia.htm
30. Galina Yaskina (1998) "Russian-Mongolian Relations: Reality and Outlook", *Far Eastern Affairs*, (5):35.
31. Sharad K. Soni (2008), "Democratic Transition in Mongolia: Achievements and Challenges ahead of 2008 Elections", *Bimonthly Journal of Mongolian and Tibetan Current Situation*, (Taipei, Taiwan), 17(1): 47-48.
32. For the full text of "Russia-Mongolia 1993 Treaty", see Appendix I.
33. Ts. Batbayar (2003), "Mongolian-Russian Relations in the Past Decade," *Asian Survey*, 43(6): 958.
34. Morris Rossabi (2005), *Modern Mongolia: From Khans to Commissars to Capitalists,* Berkeley: University of California Press. p. 201
35. Tuva, formerly known as Tannu Tuva remained under Mongol control from 13th to the first quarter of 18th centuries when it came under the Chinese. Russia recognised Chinese sovereignty over Tuva in 1757 Kiakhta treaty. However, later developments in Tuva's history led to its incorporation into the USSR in 1944. Today it is the part of Russian Federation. For more details, see Sharad K. Soni (2009), "The Siberian Republic of Tuva: Linkages with Mongolia", in Suchandana Chatterjee and others (eds.) *Asiatic Russia: Partnerships and Communities in Eurasia*, Delhi: Shipra Publications, pp.101-109.

36. Morris Rossabi (2005), *Modern Mongolia: From Khans to Commissars to Capitalists,* Berkeley: University of California Press. p203
37. Morris Rossabi (2005), *Modern Mongolia: From Khans to Commissars to Capitalists,* Berkeley: University of California Press. P. 206.
39. Ts. Batbayar (2003), "Mongolian-Russian Relations in the Past Decade," *Asian Survey*, 43(6): 964.
39. The two Presidents discussed issues concerning "the supply of Russian oil and petroleum products to Mongolia; the imposition of tariff and non-tariff barriers set against traditional Mongolian exports to Russia; the need to create a favourable legal environment for economic and border co-operation centering on local regions in the two countries; the state of military and defene relations; and the widening of access for Mongolian students to Russian educational institutions." See Ts. Batbayar, (2003), "Mongolian-Russian Relations in the Past Decade," *Asian Survey*, 43(6): 964.
40. Olivier Roy (2000), *The New Central Asia*, London and New York: I.B. Tauris), pp195-198
41. Allan M. Wachman (2009), *Mongolia's Geopolitical Gambit: Preserving a Precarious Independence While Resisting "Soft Colonialism"*, EAI Fellows Program Working Paper Series 18, Seoul: The East Asia Institute. p15
42. Ts. Batbayar (2003), "Mongolian-Russian Relations in the Past Decade," *Asian Survey*, 43(6): 965.
43. Leonid Moiseev (2001), "Relations between Russia and Mongolia are Warming", *Far Eastern Affairs*, (1): 12.
44. United Nations General Assembly (2000), *The Ulaanbaatar Declaration issued upon the official visit of Mr. V. V. Putin, President of the Russian Federation on 13 and 14 November 2000 to Mongolia,* A/55/644, 24 November, New York. Also see Appendix III.
45. Sharad K. Soni (2004), "Democracy at Work: Parliamentary Elections in Mongolia," *Himalayan and Central Asian Studies*, 8(2-3): 101.
46. Ts. Batbayar (2003), "Mongolian-Russian Relations in the Past Decade," *Asian Survey*, 43(6): 970.

47. R. Bold (1994), "The Changing International Order and Mongolia's Security," The *Mongolian Journal of International Affairs* (Ulaanbaatar), (1): 10
48. Nomin Lhagvasuren (2000), "Russia seeks to restore position in Mongolia as most favoured neighbour," *Eurasia Insight*, November 17 at http://www.eurasianet.org/departments/insight/articles/eav111700.shtml.
49. Sharad K. Soni (2006), "India's New Role in East Asia: Implications for Mongolia," *The Mongolian Journal of International Affairs,* Ulaanbaatar, No.13, pp. 41.
50. ASEAN Regional Forum, "Mongolia", *Annual Security Outlook 2001* at http://www.aseanregionalforum.org/PublicLibrary/Publications/AnnualSecurityOutlook2001/Mongolia/tabid/257/Default.aspx.
51. Gunaajav Batjargal (2010), "Foreign Policy and Development," March 10 at http://www2.jiia.or.jp/en/pdf/kouenkai/2010/100319e-batjargal.pdf.
52. Batbayar, Ts. (2003), "Mongolian-Russian Relations in the Past Decade," *Asian Survey*, 43(6): 966.
53. The Shanghai Five regional grouping was created in 1996 from the endeavour by China, Russia, and the three Central Asian Republics of Kazakhstan, Kyrgyzstan and Tajikistan to strengthen confidence-building and disarmament in the border regions. Its name was changed as Shanghai Cooperation Organisation (SCO) in 2001 after Uzbekistan was admitted as its member. Mongolia has an observer status in the SCO since 2004 followed by Pakistan, India and Iran.
54. Embassy of Mongolia in the United States of America (2010), "Foreign Policy", 8th June, URL: http://www.mongolianembassy.us/government_and_policy/foreign_policy.
55. M. Dugersuren (1994), "Changing Mongolia in a New Environment", The *Mongolian Journal of International Affairs* (Ulaanbaatar), No. 1, p. 21.
56. D. Bayarkhuu (1999), "A New World Order in the Asia-Pacific Region: A Mongolian Perspective," *World Affairs*, 3(4):101.

57. Sharad K. Soni, (2001), "Mongolia's Foreign Policy Priorities," *Himalayan and Central Asian Studies*, 5(1): 62.
58. Nambaryn Enkhbayar (2008), "Mongolia's Foreign Policy: Efforts towards Regional Peace and Security", Speech delivered at the Center for Strategic and International Studies, Washington DC, USA, *The Mongolian Journal of Strategic Studies*, Ulaanbaatar, No. 2, 8 February, p. 6.
59. G. Tumurchuluun (1999), "Mongolia's Foreign Policy Revisited: Relations with Russia and PRC into the 1990s", in Stephen Kotkin and Bruce A. Elleman, eds., *Mongolia in the Twentieth Century: Landlocked Cosmopolitan*, Armonk, New York: M.E. Sharpe, p.282.

3

Economic Co-operation

Economic activity in Mongolia has traditionally been based on herding and agriculture despite having extensive mineral deposits, like copper, coal, molybdenum, tin, tungsten and gold which account for a large part of industrial production and foreign direct investment.[1] In the pre-1991 period, particularly between 1948 and 1990 the socio-economic development of Mongolia took place under a series of five-year plans, with large scale assistance coming from the former Soviet Union and other socialist bloc countries, especially those belonging to the Council for Mutual Economic Assistance (CMEA).[2] However, changes accelerated dramatically in 1991 following the disintegration of the Soviet Union which witnessed termination of Mongolia's subsidy, withdrawal of Soviet assistance and collapse of the CMEA. As a result, Mongolia also lost her exports market as well as sources of imports. As such in the beginning of 1990s, Mongolia decided to follow the example of Russia and adopted a strategy of "shock therapy" to effect a transition from central planning to a market oriented economic system.[3] In practice "shock therapy" in Mongolia consisted of four elements: (i) Macro economic stabilisation, (ii) rapid price liberalisation (iii) wholesale privatisation of state and collectively owned assets, and (iv) non-intervention by government in the economy. In fact, the purpose of shock therapy in Mongolia was not only to bring about systemic changes but also to initiate a process of long term economic development.[4]

In such a situation mentioned above, a key factor that can not be ignored is Mongolia's landlocked geographical position. It is well known that the external economic relations of the landlocked states still depend on their neighbours for economic transactions with the outside world. Dick Hodder has rightly characterised the situation of landlocked countries as being in the state of "double dependency".[5] That is to say that their dependency arises out of twin factors: firstly, they rely on other states for access to the sea and secondly, they are dependent on other states due to their being in the category of least developed countries. Access routes to the sea have been denied to landlocked states by border closures incidental to the relationship between landlocked states and access states. The legal position in the international law on the issue of rights of landlocked states vis-a-vis transit states is also "highly complex and by no means generally agreed".[6] The same may be true in the case of Mongolia as well, and hence the following paragraphs highlights the extent and pattern of economic and trade relations between Mongolia and Russia by taking in to consideration the overall economic situation in the landlocked state of Mongolia during the period of this study.

Post-1991 Mongolia's Economic Situation

As already mentioned the collapse of the Soviet Union and the dissolution of the Trading Bloc of the Communist Economies (COMECON) or the CMEA left Mongolia with a debt to Russia of US dollar 11 billion. It was more so because Soviet investment and subsidised deliveries of raw materials came to be ceased, besides shrinking of industrial output due to the shortages of electricity, raw materials and spare parts. What one could find is that over the past 15 years or so, the Mongolian economy has undergone major structural changes. The old centrally planned economic system has been abolished and different measures have been taken towards privatisation, price liberalisation, banking reform, trade liberalisation, and opening up the economy.[7] On the external level, Mongolia had no way but to bank upon China despite the fact that the most prominent mutual interest between Russia and Mongolia was perhaps the desire to counter Chinese influence physically in Mongolia. Even Russia's strategic aim was to retain its stature as the major regional, political and economic power in Mongolia. All this together with economic necessity prompted Mongolian leaders to reorient towards Russia, which saw silver lining only after Russian President Vladimir Putin visited Mongolia in 2000.

Mongolian officials were very pleased with Putin's visit, and were anxious for Russia to once again develop economic and trade relations, though Mongolian desire was not so much in favour of reducing trade with China. Lhagvasuren (2000) notes the observation made by Sanj Bayar, the then head of the staff office of the Mongolian President, that "the objective and subjective consequences of sweeping political and economic changes in Russia and Mongolia are reasons for the slow-down of our ties in all spheres that created an unnatural vacuum in the Mongolian-Russian Relations and now with the visit of the Russian President we have a chance to balance our relations with Russia and China".[8] All these point to the fact that Mongolia's economy continued to be heavily influenced by its two neighbours. Even today Mongolia purchases 95 per cent of its petroleum products and a substantial amount of electric power from Russia, leaving it vulnerable to price increases. On the other hand, trade with China represents more than half of Mongolia's total external trade as evident from the fact that China receives about 70 per cent of Mongolia's exports. However, domestic economic situation began to improve when both Russia and China sought to improve their economic and trade relations with Mongolia through a series of agreements. Russia, in particular, began to show soft attitude towards Mongolia since the visit of Putin that also brought rays of hope for negotiation on debt issue.[9] Finally, Mongolia settled its debt with Russians at the end of 2003 on favourable terms. The Russians waived the debt in return for an immediate payment of US dollar 250 million from the Mongolian government, which issued bonds to cover part of the costs.[10]

Earlier, in late 1980s, Mongolia embarked on an economic reform to transform itself from a centrally planned to a market economy. The reforms were initiated under the direct impact of the Soviet Policy of *glasnost* and *perestroika* (in Mongolian, *iltod and orchilan baigalalt)*. However, despite the progress on the privatisation front, Mongolia had not created a market economy till 1993. The collapse of COMECON in 1990-91 had a severe impact on Mongolia's economy ending investment programmes and subsidised deliveries of raw materials, spare parts and consumer goods.[11] A shortage of foreign exchange reduced oil deliveries and damaged transport and energy production. The external economic shocks resulted in a rapid and substantial decline of the country's GDP.[12] While the GDP per capita contracted at the rate of 4 per cent annually between 1990 and 1995, it further reduced at the rate of 1.6 per cent per annum between 1996 and 2000.[13] Economic growth, thus, had been constrained by the lack of diversification in the economy, which remained dependent on mineral resources and animal husbandry.

Although agricultural production accounted for one third of the total output in the economy, it was not self sufficient to meet the demands for food. Besides, agricultural activities remained highly vulnerable due to severe weather condition. Mongolia's geographical location too contributed much to make it remote from its markets and suppliers as the access cost was relatively high due to the high dependency on transit states for access to the sea, international gateways and local markets. As a result, there were acute shortages of foodstuffs, medical supplies, basic consumer goods and essential industrial equipment.[14] Hence, Mongolia formulated transit development strategies that helped it to become more "land limbed" than land locked. Meanwhile, in 1997, the ruling Democratic Coalition (DC) government simplified tax regime and introduced value added tax that proved to be a radical step towards new privatisation revenue.[15] The initial steps in the transition to the market economy enabled positive economic growth and reduction of the inflation rate to single digit levels thus the GDP growth rate increased to 5 per cent.

Despite the fact that the transition of the economy to a market based regime has had a positive result, the progress was still slow between 1995 and 2000. Since the development of Mongolian economy has been heavily dependent on energy supply, low and controlled prices, as well as subsidised services endangered the financial viability of the energy enterprises and subsequently resulted in the introduction of inefficiencies in the economy. Therefore, it became necessary to speed up reforms in the fuel and energy sector, promote foreign and domestic direct investments, carry out privatisation, build competence and improve management of energy companies. It was also required to devise a plan in order to increase the economic efficiency of the country in accordance with the government action plan. What was basically planned to achieve was the "economic security" which was reflected in several opinion polls held in Mongolia at that point of time.[16]

In this context it can be mentioned that basically Mongolia's national security concept defines country's security not only in term of nation's "self-defense capacity but its capacity to survive and compete".[17] While this concept is the guiding principle behind factoring in a comprehensive and broadest possible range of human and national security dimensions, yet it very rightly regards economic security as "the corner stone of the independence and sovereignty of Mongolia".[18] This understanding of the importance of economics in overall national security finds greater coherence in Mongolia's foreign trade policy, the primary objective of which is to contribute to ensuring the national security by preventing negative phenomenon such as becoming a raw material supply base of another country or falling under the pressure of an international organisation or any other resulting in dependency from or domination of them. Since dependence on Russia and China cannot be ignored, Mongolia paid great attention on developing economic ties with the "third neighbours",[19] in the hope of strengthening, expanding and diversifying its international trade in order to keep a balance over two immediate neighbours. Trade liberalisation which formed a part of the economic reforms of 1990s was, therefore, aimed at not only diversifying its export and import destinations but also preventing any kind of dependency on external power.[20] However, for a smaller country like Mongolia, economic and trade relations with Russia has always been a necessity, especially to curtail Chinese monopolisation of Mongolia's international trade.

Extent and Pattern of Bilateral Trade

As already discussed, traditionally the main economic activity in Mongolia has been on agriculture and livestock with some mineral products. However, these economic activities were dominated by the Soviet policies until 1990 when Mongolia embarked on a set of political and economic reforms. Since then Mongolia has made significant efforts in achieving macroeconomic stability and fundamental structural reforms.[21] This also provided conditions for multifaceted economic and trade relations with the outside world.[22] In 1991, Mongolia became a member of international financial institutions, such as the World Bank (WB) and the International Monetary Fund (IMF), followed by the joining of the World Trade Organisation (WTO) in 1997. At the beginning of the economic reforms, trade reforms and liberalisation were aimed at integration with international trade as part of Mongolia's initial economic transformation policy, which was formulated in the light of the country's immediate priority of establishing the basis for a market economy. Therefore, along with eliminating the state monopoly, the government abolished all quantitative restrictions on exports and imports since the early 1990s, along with the state order system for exports and imports.[23]

In order to give boost to privatisation efforts, all forms of economic entity were permitted, including sole proprietorships, with individuals being allowed to engage freely in independent foreign trade activities in accordance with the Law of Mongolia on Economic Entities (or Company), which came into effect on July 1, 1991.[24] Since all former state-owned trading firms were privatised in the early 1990s, virtually all foreign trade activities in Mongolia began to be handled by private companies and individuals.[25] Throughout the period of transition, successive Mongolian governments pursued various trade liberalisation policies in the hope of strengthening and expanding international trade. As such in 1997, Mongolia abolished customs duties and excise taxes on all imported goods, with the exception of alcohol, tobacco, petroleum and motor vehicles (Jeffries 2001:306). Mongolian trade also suffered from sharp falls in the world prices for copper, gold and cashmere, and so earnings from these leading export products plunged. This caused a ripple effect that resulted in various budget problems, a decline in the national currency and a general disruption of macroeconomic stability giving rise to the largest deficit since the collapse of the former Soviet Union. In response to these problems, Mongolia adopted several measures to increase budget revenues by introducing Value Added Tax Law in 1998 and reinstating a 5 per cent uniform import tariff with exceptions for a few goods.[26]

During the period of this study, it has been revealed that although Mongolia heavily relied on international trade, its export base was narrow and commodity-based. A large proportion of its total exports consisted of just a few products. The main export commodities included copper and molybdenum, copper and spar concentrates, animals and animal products, wool and wool products, as well as cashmere and cashmere products. On the other hand, import commodities included some food items, diesel, petroleum products, and industrial equipment. As copper is the most important export product, Mongolia's export performance was highly sensitive to copper price fluctuations. Together with gold, these two products accounted for more than half of Mongolia's total export. Although Mongolia's total trade turnover increased each year after the introduction of Value Added Tax Law in 1998, foreign trade balance remained negative, mainly due to the world price decrease of its key export products such as copper, gold and cashmere. **Table 1** shows the negative trends in Mongolia's trade balance during the period from 1999 to 2001.

Table 1: Mongolia's Trade Balance, 1999-2001

(In US $ million)	*1999*	*2000*	*2001*
Trade balance	–113.1	–140.2	–169.9
Exports	457.2	535.8	523.2
Imports	567.3	676.0	693.1

Source: Zolbayar Chuluunbat (2006), "Mongolia", *International Comparisons of Taxation in Developing Countries*, at http://www.ic.keio.ac.jp/en/download/jjwbgsp/2006/4_Mongolia.pdf.

Significantly, Mongolia became less dependent on Europe, specifically Russia, for its trade turnover. While comparing the trade figures with the two neighbours it has been found that trade with Russia consistently decreased since 1990 as compared to China which emerged as the largest trading partner.[27] Yet, Russia remained a key trading partner even during the transitional period because of Mongolia's continued dependence of energy imports from Russia and the joint Mongolian and Russian ownership of the large Erdenet Copper mine.[28] The pattern of Mongolia-Russia bilateral trade underlines the fact that a comprehensive cooperation with Russia has been a natural choice for Mongolia in pursuing its national interests. In this regard, Mongolia considered three main concerns.[29] Firstly, geopolitical relationship with Russia has always been an important element of Mongolia's security. Secondly, Mongolia keeps in mind Russia's importance as its partner especially since it needs Russia for the supply of energy. And thirdly, Russia's role as a heavyweight in Eurasia is of great value to Mongolia as it seeks to be connected to Europe. The last concern is more important for Mongolia as it has created stable interactions with the European Union and other international organisations since the 1990s.

In fact, it was on January 1, 1991 that Mongolia and the former Soviet Union agreed to conduct their bilateral trade in hard currency at wolrd prices. For the first half of 1991, while Mongolian exports to the former Soviet Union amounted to US $110 million, the total amount for imports reached at US$97 million. During the visit of the Mongolian Prime Minister Byambasuren to Moscow in 1991, an important protocol on economic cooperation was disseminated which called for the resolution of crucial problems, such as Mongolia's debt to the Soviet Union, the need to improve the activities of joint Soviet-Mongolian economic entities in Mongolia, and the termination of Mongolia-based Soviet construction projects with a transfer of their production funds to the Mongolian side.[30]

However, a mutual trading clearance regime with hard-currency payment appeared to have not workable for either side as it is evident from the fact that Mongolia delivered goods worth US $50 million to Russia, but trade had to be temporarily suspended because Moscow had failed to pay for them. The 39th session of the Mongolian-Russian Intergovernmental Committee, held in Moscow in July 1992, then decided to adopt a special accounting method for bilateral trade. Whereas Mongolian exports to Russia consisted mostly of minerals (copper and fluorspar) and meat products, leather goods and carpets, the imports from Russia included mostly oil and petroleum products required for the well-being of Mongolia's economy (Chang 1998:252).

Furthermore, almost 80 per cent of Mongolia's imports from Russia included oil and petroleum products, on which

Mongolia continued to depend in addition to the delivery of Russian spare parts for Mongolian enterprises, in particular, for thermo-power stations, which were built with Soviet assistance.[31] In 1992, Mongolia and Russia held their first meeting on trade, economic, scientific, and technological cooperation.[32] The meeting culminated in signing of a protocol between the two sides on trade and economic cooperation as well as an agreement which allowed for the postponement of Mongolia's 1991-95 debt repayment until the year 2000 on an interest-free basis.[33] The year 1993 saw somehow a triumph over disruption in Mongolia's foreign trade during the initial period of early 1990s, especially slimming down of Mongolia's imports. As a result, a surge in Mongolia's imports was recorded in 1995, though the overall trade figure was not encouraging.[34] The government statistics reveal that Mongolia's total imports that year were valued at US $ 415.3 million, including those from Russia at a total of US $ 208 million.[35] Similarly, Mongolia's exports in 1995 were valued at US $ 473.3 million, including US $ 68.9 million of those to Russia (Table 2).

Mineral products, including copper and fluorspar concentrate, accounted for about two-thirds of Mongolia's total exports, while petroleum products, including petrol, diesel, jet fuel, and lubricants, accounted for about 20 per cent of Mongolia's total imports in the same year.[36] Whereas in the pre-1990 period over 90 per cent of Mongolia's foreign trade was with the former Soviet Union and Eastern European countries, by 1995 the equation changed so much so that 54.1 per cent of Mongolia's exports were redirected to neighbouring countries in East Asia, 24.5 per cent to Western Europe, and the remainder to Eastern Europe.[37] On the other hand, Mongolia's trade with China and other East Asian countries registered a faster growth mainly due to normalisation of Sino-Mongolian relations which was perhaps a direct result of China's new periphery policy.[38] Besides, Mongolia too came to understand that its "destiny is no longer an exclusive object of dispute between Russia and

China", rather "economics are increasingly the dominant force in its international relations".[39]

Table 2: Mongolia's Exports to Major Destinations, 1985-2000 (In US $ million)

	1985	*1990*	*1995*	*2000*
China	2.7 (0.4%)	11.3 (1.7%)	77.8 (16.4%)	274.3 (51.2%)
Former Soviet Union*	530.7 (77.0%)	517.5 (78.3%)	NA	NA
Russia	NA	NA	68.9 (14.6%)	45.1 (8.4%)
USA	0.1 (0.01%)	0.9 (0.1%)	25.8 (5.5%)	130.2 (24.3%)
ROK	NA	NA	26.1 (5.5%)	12.2 (2.3%)
Japan	7.4 (1.1%)	7.6 (1.2%)	46.7 (9.9%)	8.1 (1.5%)
Australia	NA	NA	NA	12.5 (2.3%)
Singapore	NA	NA	1.8 (0.4%)	0.1 (0.01%)
Germany	24.3 (3.5%)	13.7 (2.1%)	7.6 (1.6%)	2.0 (0.4%)
UK	2.8 (0.4%)	3.0 (0.5%)	18.7 (4.0%)	17.5 (3.3%)
Others	120.9 (17.5%)	106.7 (16.1%)	199.9 (42.2%)	33.8 (6.3%)
Total	**689.1**	**660.7**	**473.3**	**535.8**

Notes:

1. *Data for FSU includes Russia and other former republics i.e. the members of the Commonwealth of Independent States (CIS), such as Ukraine, Kazakhstan and Georgia
2. NA Indicates that there are no records;
3. Numbers in parentheses are total shares;

Source: National Statistical Office, *Mongolian Statistical Yearbook*, various issues, Ulaanbaatar.

Bilateral trade in natural resources constituted the centerpiece of Mongolia-Russia economic relations. For example, in 1995, copper accounted for 73.5 per cent of Mongolia's exports to Russia, while oil and petroleum products accounted for 21.4 per cent of imports from Russia. Because of hard-currency shortages on both sides, barter trade was of great importance as this amounted to 35 per cent of two-way trade that year as negotiated during the visit of the Mongolian Prime Minister P. Jasrai to Moscow.[40]

Table 3: Trade between Mongolia and Major Trading Partners (In US$ million)

Country	*1999*		*2000*	
China	**285.8**		**400.1**	
	Export	208.2	Export	274.3
	Import	77.6	Import	125.8
Russia	**198.8**		**251.3**	
	Export	48.2	Export	45.1
	Import	149.8	Import	206.2
US	**109.5**		**158.6**	
	Export	78.0	Export	130.2
	Import	31.5	Import	28.4
Japan	**125.9**		**81.4**	
	Export	10.9	Export	8.1
	Import	115.0	Import	73.3

Sources: National Statistical Office (1998), *Mongolian Statistical Yearbook-1997*, Ulan-Bator, 1998, 210-215; National Statistical Office (2001), *Mongolian Statistical Yearbook-2000*, Ulaanbaatar, 178, 180.

During this visit both sides signed nearly a dozen agreements in various areas including the economic and trade spheres. The two countries also underlined the importance of the Russian supply of oil and petroleum products to Mongolia by including the items in the annual agreement on trade and economic cooperation. However, as shown in **Table 2, Table**

3 and Table 6, Mongolia's export volume to Russia continued to decline during the entire period of 1990s, thereby affecting the overall trade volume between the two sides.[41] The reason behind such stagnation in their bilateral trade was "high Russian customs and transit tariffs and inefficiencies that plagued Russian enterprises tied to the Mongolian market.[42] However, Russia remained the major source of imports to Mongolia, despite having lost its leading share in total trade turnover **(Table 4).**

Table 4: Mongolia's Imports from Major Partners, 1985-2000 (In US $ million)

	1985	*1990*	*1995*	*2000*
China	4.9 (0.4%)	22.3 (2.4%)	44.5 (10.7%)	125.8 (20.5%)
Former Soviet Union*	951.6 (86.9%)	716.2 (77.5%)	NA	NA
Russia	NA	NA	208.0 (50.1%)	206.2 (33.6%)
USA	NA	NA	14.5 (3.5%)	28.4 (4.6%)
ROK	NA	0.9 (0.1%)	21.5 (5.2%)	55.6 (9.0%)
Japan	1.8 (0.2%)	9.8 (1.1%)	45.3 (10.9%)	73.3 (11.9%)
Australia	NA	NA	NA	1.3 (0.2%)
Singapore	NA	0.7 (0.1%)	7.4 (1.8%)	10.6 (1.7%)
Germany	29.7 (2.7%)	37.4 (4.0%)	18.5 (4.5%)	29.7 (4.8%)
UK	0.7 (0.1%)	2.5 (0.3%)	2.7 (0.7%)	6.0 (1.0%)

(cont...)

Others	106.8 (9.7%)	134.2 (14.5%)	52.9 (12.7 %)	77.6 (12.6 %)
Total	**1095.5**	**924.0**	**415.3**	**614.5**

Notes:

1. *Data for FSU includes Russia and other former republics, i.e., the members of the Commonwealth of Independent States (CIS), such as Ukraine, Kazakhstan and Georgia;
2. NA Indicates that there are no records;
3. Numbers in parentheses are total shares;

Source: National Statistical Office, *Mongolian Statistical Yearbook*, various issues, Ulaanbaatar.

Yet, considering various sources when we take the average trade figure between Mongolia and Russia, it has been revealed that since the year 2000 the negative downward trend of the early and mid 1990s has been diminishing and the Russian big business has already begun to turn its eyes to Mongolia. Evidently, while in 1990, the annual trade turnover between the two sides remained at US $ 800 million, it fell in 1994 to US $ 200 million, but in 1995 it again regained to reach at US $ 277 million, which further increased to US $ 319 in 1997 and US $ 396 in 2000, the bulk of which were Russian petrochemical exports. Following the signing of the Ulaanbaatar Declaration the extent of growth in trade between the two sides can be gauged from the fact that within few years particularly in 2006 bilateral trade reached at US$ 592.9 million or nearly 75 per cent up from the 2000 figure.[43] **Table 5** highlights gradual decrease in Mongolia's export to Russia and sluggish as well as fluctuating growth in Mongolia's import from Russia. It indicates that internal needs of both countries during that period had not been very complementary.

It is also to be noted that during Putin's visit to Mongolia in 2000, the Russian side expressed interest in resuming cooperation in the agricultural sphere apart from participating in the privatisation of selected Mongolian enterprises.

Table 5: Mongolia's Trade with Russia, 1991-2001 (Value in US $ million and % Share of World)

	1991	*1992*	*1993*	*1994*	*1995*	*1996*	*1997*	*1998*	*1999*	*2000*	*2001*
Mongolia's Exports to World:	67.39	388.4	382.66	356.1	473.27	424.29	451.54	345.14	358.29	535.83	521.44
Mongolia's Exports to Russia	NA	219.7	145.23	108.8	68.9	87.55	46.64	40.59	48.22	45.15	44.94
% Share of World		**56.57**	**37.95**	**30.55**	**14.56**	**20.63**	**10.33**	**11.76**	**13.46**	**8.43**	**8.62**
Mongolia's Imports from World:	162.8	418.3	379.01	258.4	415.31	450.94	468.26	503.28	512.75	614.46	637.74
Mongolia's Imports from Russia	NA	214.3	220.28	148.8	208.02	154.91	165.94	150.24	149.82	206.23	225.96
% Share of World		**51.23**	**58.12**	**57.59**	**50.09**	**34.35**	**35.44**	**29.85**	**29.22**	**33.56**	**35.43**

Source: International Monetary Fund (IMF), *Direction of Trade Statistics Yearbook*, CDROM-2009, Washington DC.

Putin affirmed that Russia understood the current dire economic situation of Mongolia and would not, therefore, press the debt issue. He promised to find the ways to resolve this problem without adversely affecting the future development of the Mongolian economy. Thus the issue of international energy projects was also given prominence. Mongolia was interested in the transit of oil and in gas pipeline routes passing through its territory, and in a power-transmission line to be built between Russia and China. The 2000 Ulaanbaatar Declaration underscored the importance the two countries attached to these major energy projects in Northeast Asia. Russia expressed its support for Mongolia's participation because of Mongolia's strategic location.[44]

Table 6: Mongolia's Major Trade Partners (Export-wise), 1990-2000 (In US$ million)

Ranking	*Country*	*1990*	*1995*	*1999*	*2000*
1	China	33.6	122.3	285.8	400.1
	*Hong Kong	2.7	9.1	NA	NA
	Soviet Union	1233.7	NA	NA	NA
2	**Russia**	**NA**	**276.9**	**198**	**251.3**
3	USA	0.9	40.3	77.8	121.3
4	Japan	17.4	92	125.9	81.4
5	South Korea	0.7	47.6	38.3	58.3
6	Germany	51.1	26.1	26	31.6
7	Italy	9.1	15	19.1	17.5
8	UK	5.5	21.4	17.5	17.2
9	Singapore	0.7	9.2	10	10.7
10	France	5.1	2.1	9.2	10.1
11	Kazakhstan	NA	75.2	1	7.8
12	Netherlands	1.6	5.2	4.7	6.1
13	Poland	24.4	1.1	4.5	4.8
14	Denmark	0.1	4.1	3	4.4
15	Byelorussia	NA	NA	2.4	4.2
16	Belgium	0.4	3.1	2.9	4
17	Switzerland	7.1	83	2.9	4

(cont...)

18	Bulgaria	33.7	0.6	3.2	3.6
	Czech-Slovak	63.9	NA	NA	NA
19	Czech Rep.	NA	10.3	5	3.5
20	Austria	10	5.7	0.4	1.9
21	Hungary	34.2	0.5	1.4	1.7
22	Afghanistan	1.5	0.1	NA	0.7
23	North Korea	13.3	0.3	0.2	0
24	Romania	16.4	0.1	0	0
	Total	**1584.7**	**888.6**	**871.1**	**1080.6**

Source: National Statistical Office (2001). *Mongolian Statistical Yearbook-2000*, Ulaanbaatar, 177.

*Hong Kong statistics after 1997 are incorporated into China.

In terms of investments, in 1992, Russia agreed to provide US $ 38.6 million in loans for the purpose of construction in Mongolia.[45] This was followed by a Russian grant of US $ 38.75 million loan to Mongolia for its extension of power and civil construction works, out of which contracts worth US $ 35.78 million were signed and their realisation constituted US $ 32.26 million as of December 1, 1994.[46] Besides, US $ 13.35 million for the financing of construction and installation of 11 projects were also agreed upon in the same year. Thus the year 1994 was marked by first positive shifts in the economy of the country in its tough and irreversible movement towards market-oriented system.[47] However, throughout the 1990s China topped the list of investors in Mongolia as it is evident from the fact that between 1994 and 2004 Chinese investment made up 40 per cent of total foreign direct investment (FDI) in Mongolia.[48]

As regards border trade, Siberian regions are responsible for 70 per cent of Russia's overall trade with Mongolia, including some 80 per cent of Russian exports. The Irkutsk region is responsible for some 60 per cent of Russia's trade with Mongolia.[49] During the period of this study, Irkutsk oblast alone was the sole exporter of oil and petroleum products as well as electricity to neighbouring Mongolia.

Mineral extraction and the geological projects had long encouraged cross-border cooperation between Mongolia and Russia. Over 200 new joint ventures were established in Mongolia with the participation of those Russian regions, particularly in construction works, machine and agricultural vehicle repair, as well as processing of agricultural raw materials. While Buryatia Republic opened its office in Ulaanbaatar, Irkutsk oblast established a trading center in the Mongolia capital. Various Russian governors in Siberia had previously established an interregional association based on a Siberia Agreement. The association lobbied hard to get the Kremlin to endorse cross-border economic and commercial interactions. Those governors were also interested primarily in reviving economic and trade ties with Mongolia in order to invigorate their ailing industries.

In addition, Mongolia and Russia represented big business interests in each other, especially in the energy sector. In 1999, when the Mongolian President visited Moscow to have a meeting with the Russian President Boris Yeltsin, the two sides discussed several issues including the supply of Russian oil and petroleum products to Mongolia as well as creating a favourable legal environment for carrying out the border trade.[50] Soon representatives of the Russian *Yukos* company visited Mongolia to sign a memorandum with the Mongolia Ministry of Infrastructure concerning the future oil and gas pipeline. Another Russian energy giant, *Gazprom*, negotiated with the government in Ulaanbaatar to build gas stations in Mongolia in order to establish a network for natural gas consumption in the country.[51] Even then economic and trade relationship between the two countries was "handicapped by the problem of transportation in the border areas".[52]

Post-2000 Scenario in Economic Co-operation

Until 2000, Mongolia-Russia trade basically reflects the common trend in the course of economic transformation: democracy politically and free-market economically, besides extending international cooperation in the areas of economy and technology. As such, Zhao (2005) argues that Mongolia-Russia bilateral relationship has been affected to a large extent by the situation in international relations in the Far East region, including relationships between Russia and China, Mongolia and China, and even the triangular relationship between Russia, Mongolia, and China in the areas of border, diplomacy, economic security, etc. Going beyond the year 2000, it has been found that Mongolia's trade with Russia has experienced continued deficits, accounting for US $ 224.2 million in 2003. This large trade deficit was associated with the fact that Mongolia imported 93 per cent of the petroleum and 97 per cent of the diesel fuel consumed in 2003 from Russia. Due to increasing oil prices and domestic demand for petroleum and petroleum products, the trade deficit with Russia increased further.[53] Trade between East European bloc and Mongolia plummeted at the end of Cold War, largely due to reconstruction of East European economies which directly affected trade with Mongolia. China, with the advantage of geographical proximity, easily became Mongolia's largest trade partner after 1999.[54]

Throughout the 1990s, trade items of Mongolia were directly related to its economic production items. According to the government statistics, Mongolia's major export items in 2000 included molybdenum, large-sized livestock, sheep, knitwear, and ready-made garments, while major import items consisted of trucks, buses, small cars, burning fuel, vehicle gasoline and power.[55] Mongolia and Russia tried to raise the level of their bilateral trade, particularly after signing of the 2000 Ulaanbaatar Declaration which built a solid foundation under the bilateral relationship structure.[56] However, there have also been problems that Russia needs to address. Firstly, Russia's trade with Mongolia is still mostly initiated by local government (oblast and republic), hence it is under the heavy influence of the central government's economic and trade policies, especially the central government's attitude towards Mongolia as outlined in its foreign policies. Secondly, the gap between fundamental economic structures of the two sides is still likely to result in the lack of balance in trade development. And thirdly, there exists difference in attitude between Russia's central government and local governments so far as trade with Mongolia is concerned. As a result there has been imbalance in the economic and trade relationship between the two sides. Besides, process of trade is heavily affected by the political relationship between the central and local governments in Russia and the political situation of local governments in both Russia and Mongolia.

On the other hand, Mongolia has adequate advantages in the development of future bilateral economic and trade cooperation: it has rich proven mineral resources, including gold, copper, molybdenum, and fluorite. This, combined with Mongolia's status as an independent, sovereign nation, puts Mongolia in a good position to attract foreign investment.[57] As such, Russia's Siberia region has a unique geopolitical advantage in extending cooperation with Mongolia.[58] Furthermore, labour resources and simplified entry and exit procedures would certainly facilitate circulation of capital and human resources in a small country like Mongolia. While there are definitely positive signs in the development of Mongolia-Russia relationship, Mongolia still has to improve some of its internal qualities, such as legal system, democratisation, and socio-economic development in order to effectively carry out its foreign and national security policies, more importantly to achieve economic security. For Russia it is more important to increase the number of joint ventures it has in Mongolia so as to maintain its influence, profits, and foreign investment.[59] Of late, Russia's efforts to improve the transportation system will create more possibilities in economic cooperation among Russia, Mongolia and China.[60]

From the above analysis, in terms of overall trends, trading partners, structure and main export and import commodities, it can be said that Mongolia's foreign trade, particularly with former Soviet Union/Russia attained its peak level in the late 1980s, but deteriorated sharply during the initial years of the country's economic transition from a centrally command economy to a market oriented one in the early 1990s. It then began to revitalise after 1995, though the pace was slow and full recovery had not been achieved until 2003 when the Mongolian Prime Minister N. Enkhbayar visited Mongolia in an effort to foster closer ties with Russia. However, after the extensive liberalisation of trade in the initial years of its economic transition, Mongolia's foreign trade diversified in terms of destinations of its exports and the sources of its imports. Exports were dominated by mineral products and those of livestock origin, whereas imports comprised a wide range of consumer products and industrial goods. But due to the collapse of the domestic leather industry, export commodities of livestock origin shifted from finished goods to raw and low value-added semi-processed materials.[61]

In the current scenario, the international relations of Mongolia has now shifted from predominantly political and military fields to economic, scientific-technological and information sectors in other words, "from geopolitics to geo-economics".[62] Economic prosperity, therefore, has become a common priority agenda for both Russia and Mongolia in order to ensure their overall security. Even Russian policy makers have indicated that only Moscow can help Mongolia to balance relations with China in the long run.[63] It is, therefore, obvious that the close connection between Russia-China and China-Mongolia relations would remain a part of the new international order.[64] Even Government of the Russian Federation has recently stated that "stagnation in Russian-Mongolian relations has been largely overcome, and they are rapidly developing now in the spirit of strategic partnership".[65] Yet, considering the fact that Russia has many domestic political and economic issues on its side, it will need to develop a set of more active and positive foreign economic policies to meet the long-term demand in Mongolia.

Only then Russia's role in Mongolia can become in future similar to that of the former Soviet Union, particularly in the economic field.

Notes and References

1. CIA-The World Fact Book (2010), "Mongolia", 24th June, URL: https://www.cia.gov/library/publications/the-world-factbook/geos/mg.html.
2. *Ibid.*
3. Morris Rossabi (2005), *Modern Mongolia: From Khans to Commissars to Capitalists,* Berkeley: University of California Press, 49. Shagdar, Enkhbayar (2007), "Neo-liberal 'Shock Therapy' Policy during Mongolian Economic Transition", ERINA Discussion Paper No. 0703e, Niigata, April, 13.
4. Keith Griffin, "Agricultural Involution and Urban to Rural Migration in Mongolia", URL: http://economics.ucr.edu/papers/papers02/02-02.pdf.
5. Dick Hodder and others (1998), *Landlocked States of Africa and Asia*, London: Frankcass publishers.210).
6. *Ibid.,* p. 211.
7. New Zealand Ministry of Foreign Affairs and Trade, "Mongolia: Country Information Paper", URL: http://www.Mfat.govt.nz./Countries/Asia-North/Mongolia.php.
8. Nomin Lhagvasuren (2000), "Russia Seeks to Restore Position in Mongolia as Most Favored Neighbor", *Eurasia Insight,* 17 November, URL: http://www.eurasianet.org/departments/insight/articles/eav111700.shtml.
9. Ts. Batbayar (2003), "Mongolian-Russian Relations in the Past Decade," *Asian Survey*, 43(6): 967.
10. Morris Rossabi (2005), *Modern Mongolia: From Khans to Commissars to Capitalists,* Berkeley: University of California Press- 210.
11. EIU (2008), "The Economy: Economic Performance", *Country Profile Mongolia 2008*, 4th April.
12. Hashbat Hulan (1994), "Mongolia's Political Transformation: Observations and Comparisons", *The Mongolian Journal of International Affairs,* (1): 32.

13. ESCAP and the United Nations Development Programme (2003), *Promoting the Millennium Development Goals in Asia and the Pacific: Meeting the Challenges of Poverty Reduction*, United Nations Publication, ST/ESCAP/2253, Sales No. F.03.II.F.29.
14. Hulan , "Mongolia's Political Transformation: Observations and Comparisons".
15. EIU (2008), "The Economy: Economic Performance", *Country Profile Mongolia 2008*, 4th April.
16. The most pressing security problem for Mongolia then was the economic security, see Interview with the *Mongol Messenger* of J. Enkhsaikhan, Secretary of Mongolia's National Security Council, *The Mongolian Journal of International* Affairs (1994), (1): 71.
17. R. Bold (2000), *The Security of Small State: Option for Mongolia*, Ulaanbaatar: The Institute for Strategic Studies;36; Soni, Sharad K. (2006), *Mongolia-China Relations: Modern and Contemporary Times*, New Delhi: Pentagon Press. 228
18. Wayne Nelles (2000), "Reconciling Human and National Security in Mongolia: A Canadian Perspective", Programme on Canada-Asia Policy Studies, Institute of Asian Research, University of British-Columbia, North Pacific Policy Paper 10.
19. In 2005, Mongolia's Foreign Minister Ts. Munh-Orgil described the "third neighbours" as the collective community of democracies supporting Mongolia's transformation to a political democracy and market economy. See Ts. Munh-Orgil (2005), Regional Integration Processes and Mongolia", *The Mongolian Journal of International Affairs*, (12): 5.
20. M.A. Dorsey (2001), "The International Mongolian Economy: The Transition from. 5p).
21. Zolbayar Chuluunbat (2006), "Mongolia", *International Comparisons of Taxation in Developing Countries*, URL: http://www.ic.keio.ac.jp/en/download/jjwbgsp/2006/4_Mongolia.pdf).
22. O. Nyamdavaa (2001), "Mongolia-India Relations: Some Perspectives", *Himalayan and Central Asian Studies*, 5(1): 19-32.

23. Enkhbayar Shagdar (2005), "Mongolia's Foreign Trade,1985-2003", ERINA Report, March, 62: 1.
24. Georges Korsun and Peter Mirrell (1995), "Politics and Economics of Mongolia's Privatisation Program", *Asian Survey*, 35(5): 479.
25. Enkhbayar Shagdar (2005), "Mongolia's Foreign Trade,1985-2003", *ERINA Report*, March, 62:1-2.
26. IMF (2000), *Mongolia: Statistical Annex*, Staff Country Report No. 00/26, 6 March, 49, URL: http://www.imf.org/external/pubs/ft/scr/2000/cr0026.pdf
27. Sharad K. Soni (2009), "China's Periphery Policy: Implications for Sino-Mongolian Relations", *India Quarterly,* 65(3): 258.
28. Alan J.K. Sanders (1987), *Mongolia: Politics, Economics and Society*, London: Frances Pinter. p.87.
29. Zhu-cheng Zhao, (2005), "Mongolian Economic Security Policies toward Russia, 1990- 2000", *Bimonthly Journal of Mongolian and Tibetan Current Situation* (Taipei, Taiwan), 14 (2), March: 9.
30. Ts. Batbayar (2003), "Mongolian-Russian Relations in the Past Decade," *Asian Survey*, 43(6): 956.
31. See Ts. Batbayar (1993), "Mongolia in 1992: Back to One-Party Rule", *Asian Survey*, 33 (1):61-66.
32. G. Tumurchuluun (1999), "Mongolia's Foreign Policy Revisited: Relations with Russia and PRC into the 1990s", in Stephen Kotkin and Bruce A. Elleman, eds., *Mongolia in the Twentieth Century: Landlocked Cosmopolitan*, Armonk, New York: M.E.Sharpe, 281.
33. Ts. Batbayar (1993), "Mongolia in 1992: Back to One-Party Rule", *Asian Survey*, 33 (1):64.
34. Morris Rossabi (2005), *Modern Mongolia: From Khans to Commissars to Capitalists,* Berkeley: University of California Press. p.202.
35. See National Statistical Office (2001), *Mongolian Statistical Yearbook 2000*, Ulaanbaatar, pp.177-185.
36. *Ibid.*

37. Ts. Batbayar (2003), "Mongolian-Russian Relations in the Past Decade," *Asian Survey*, 43(6): 959
38. Sharad K. Soni (2009), "China's Periphery Policy: Implications for Sino-Mongolian Relations", *India Quarterly,* 65(3)pp: 258-261.
39. G. Tumurchuluun (1999), "Mongolia's Foreign Policy Revisited: Relations with Russia and PRC into the 1990s", in Stephen Kotkin and Bruce A. Elleman, eds., *Mongolia in the Twentieth Century: Landlocked Cosmopolitan*, Armonk, New York: M.E.Sharpe, pp286-287.
40. Ts. Batbayar (2003), "Mongolian-Russian Relations in the Past Decade," *Asian Survey*, 43(6): 960.
41. Morris Rossabi (2005), *Modern Mongolia*: *From Khans to Commissars to Capitalists,* Berkeley: University of California Press. p.202.
42. Ts. Batbayar (2003), "Mongolian-Russian Relations in the Past Decade," *Asian Survey*, 43(6): 965.
43. Sergei Blagov (2008), "Moscow Seeks to Engage Mongolia Economic Ally", *Eurasia Daily Monitor*, April 24, URL: http://www.jamestown.org/edm/email-to-friend.php?article_id=2373002.
44. See United Nations General Assembly (2000), *The Ulaanbaatar Declaration issued upon the official visit of Mr. V. V. Putin, President of the Russian Federation on 13 and 14 November 2000 to Mongolia,* A/55/644, 24th November, New York. Also see Appendix III.
45. G. Tumurchuluun (1999), "Mongolia's Foreign Policy Revisited: Relations with Russia and PRC into the 1990s", in Stephen Kotkin and Bruce A. Elleman, eds., *Mongolia in the Twentieth Century: Landlocked Cosmopolitan*, Armonk, New York: M.E.Sharpe, 281.
46. Mongolian Chamber of Commerce and Industry, "Review of the Mongolian Economy for 1994", URL: http://www.indiana.edu/~mongsoc/mong/review.htm
47. *Ibid.*
48. Narangoa 2009: 367.

49. Sergei Blagov (2005), "Ties between Russia and Mongolia Stall", *Eurasia Daily Monitor*, February 3, URL: http://www.jamestown.org/edm/article.php?article_id=2369201
50. Ts. Batbayar (2003), "Mongolian-Russian Relations in the Past Decade," *Asian Survey*, 43(6): 964.
51. Ts. Batbayar (2003), "Mongolian-Russian Relations in the Past Decade," *Asian Survey*, 43(6): 969.
52. Ilyas Kamalov (2010), "Mongolia-Russia Relations: Some Perspectives", in K. Warikoo and Sharad K. Soni (eds.), *Mongolia in the 21st Century: Society, Culture and International Relations*, New Delhi: Pentagon Press, 240.
53. Enkhbayar Shagdar (2005), "Mongolia's Foreign Trade,1985-2003", ERINA Report, March, 62: 4.
54. Zhu-cheng Zhao (2005), "Mongolian Economic Security Policies toward Russia, 1990- 2000", *Bimonthly Journal of Mongolian and Tibetan Current Situation* (Taipei, Taiwan), 14 (2), March: 12.
55. See National Statistical Office (2001), *Mongolian Statistical Yearbook 2000*, Ulaanbaatar, pp182-183.
56. Luvsan Khaisandai (2010), "Contemporary Mongolia-Russia Relations", Kamalov, Ilyas (2010), "Mongolia-Russia Relations: Some Perspectives", in K. Warikoo and Sharad K. Soni (eds.), *Mongolia in the 21st Century: Society, Culture and International Relations*, New Delhi: Pentagon Press, p.229.
57. International Business Wiki, "Mongolia's Natural Resources", URL: http://internationalbusiness.wikia.com/wiki/Mongolia's_Natural_Resources
58. Zhu-cheng Zhao (2005), "Mongolian Economic Security Policies toward Russia, 1990- 2000", *Bimonthly Journal of Mongolian and Tibetan Current Situation* (Taipei, Taiwan), 14 (2), March: 14.
59. Morris Rossabi (2005), *Modern Mongolia: From Khans to Commissars to Capitalists,* Berkeley: University of California Press. 205.
60. Zhu-cheng Zhao (2005), "Mongolian Economic Security Policies toward Russia, 1990- 2000", *Bimonthly Journal*

of Mongolian and Tibetan Current Situation (Taipei, Taiwan), 14 (2), March: 17.

61. Enkhbayar Shagdar (2007), "Neo-liberal 'Shock Therapy' Policy during Mongolian Economic Transition", ERINA Discussion Paper no. 0703e, Niigata, April, 7.
62. J. Enkhsaikhan (1995), "Mongolia's Security Policy: Regional and International Aspects," *The Mongol Messenger*, 18 (210), 14th July.
63. Jennifer Anderson (1997), "The Limits of Sino-Russian Strategic Partnership", *Adelphi Paper*, No. 315.
64. Sharad K. Soni (2009), "China's Periphery Policy: Implications for Sino-Mongolian Relations", *India Quarterly*, 65(3): 267.
65. Government of the Russian Federation, Prime Minister of the Russian Federation, International Visits, "Russian-Mongolian Relations",13th May 2009, URL: http://www.premier.gov.ru/eng/pda/visits/world/105/info/2852.html.

4

Strategic Partnership

The right of any country to ensure its security without undermining the security of others is a well recognised fact. Mongolia is not an exception. With the end of bipolar world and search for a genuine security as well as changes in international relations in the early 1990s, Mongolia got an opportunity to free itself from the Soviet influence and redefine its vital national interests and foreign policy priorities. As discussed in the second chapter, Mongolia formulated its national security and foreign policy concepts based on its own interests. These two concepts further gave way to adopt yet another document known as the Military Doctrine, which is basically the country's defence policy. Together all the three documents directed Mongolia to chalk out its strategy for establishing strategic relationship with the outside world.

Post-1991: Mongolian Security Strategy

The content of defence policy, i.e., the security strategy of every nation is defined by the state external and internal policy, its social, political and economic system, geographical location, specifics of possible military threats, the country's defence capability as well as by level of its scientific and industrial development, and some other factors.[1] Keeping this fact in mind, in the post-1991 period "Mongolia's security concerns are aimed at achieving favourable internal and external conditions for ensuring national interests".[2] The adoption of the National Security Concept in 1992 thus was a landmark event that brought "a fundamental change in Mongolia's post-Communist security thinking as well." According to this Concept, "the vital national interests of Mongolia consist in the existence of the Mongolian people and their civilisation, in the country's independence, sovereignty, territorial integrity, inviolability of State frontiers, relative economic independence, sustainable ecological development and national unity."[3]

However, the Concept of National Security of Mongolia with regard to country's foreign relations insists that Mongolia will exercise "political realism and consistently principled approach, accord top priority to vital national interests and other national considerations, seek to secure many partners in its international relations and promote a non-aligned policy so long as it does not threaten the country's vital interests."[4] Soni (2002) argues that by pursuing an open foreign policy Mongolia is committed to "promote the policy of consultation with influential countries on issues of strengthening world peace and security, of developing international cooperation, of enhancing the country's strategic significance and fostering strategic interests of major powers in Mongolia".[5] One of the major procedures for implementing the Concept of National Security has been the State defence policy. In line with the major changes in the political, social, and economic systems, the defence policy of Mongolia has been formulated on quite a new basis in conformity to the new conditions of democracy, market economy and international relations brought about since the 1990s. The creation of a unified political, economic, social, legal, and military system to ensure the defence of the country; the modernisation of the armed forces and other troops aimed at making them professionally-oriented, compact and efficient; the strengthening of the border troops; and the prioritisation of political and diplomatic means in the defence policy of the country constitute the fundamentals of the defence policy of Mongolia reflected in the Action Program of the Government of Mongolia for the years 1996-2000.[6]

In 1993, the Mongolian Parliament adopted the Law on the Defence of Mongolia in order to facilitate establishment of an integrated defence system, determine the structure, organisation, and functions of the armed forces, and regulate relations rising from implementation of the state defence policy.[7] According to the Law on the Defence of Mongolia, the defence of Mongolia forms part of the activities to ensure the national security through complex political, economic, social, legal and military measures to defend the people, independence, sovereignty, and territorial integrity of Mongolia against foreign armed incursion and aggression. Activities directed toward ensuring the inviolability of the state frontiers of Mongolia and defending its population against natural disasters and weapons of mass destruction are a component of the state defence system. In other words, the safeguarding of state frontiers and civilian defence are included in the notion of "defence".[8]

The most important document on defence policy adopted in 1994 by the Mongolian Parliament is the "Fundamentals of the Military Doctrine of Mongolia" which was of great significance. It formulated the main directions of foreign and domestic policies in relation to a legal basis for implementing military reforms and ensuring military security. By abandoning the military policy of being part of the community of socialist countries and its obligations to defend its eastern frontiers by military means, the new military doctrine of Mongolia declared that priority shall be given to political and diplomatic means in ensuring the security of the country. The document stipulated that, "Mongolia shall develop all round, friendly relations and cooperation with the countries of the world, particularly with neighboring states, and work to bring about military trust, refrain from and/or prevent any activity that may adversely affect its vital national interests, and thereby eliminate grounds for and causes of external military threat".[9]

As elaborated in the *Mongolian Defence White Paper, 1997-1998,* the basic features of the Military Doctrine of Mongolia are defined as follows:

In pursuing its peace-loving policy of creating favourable external conditions for ensuring national security and preventing any threat of war and aggression in conformity with universally recognised principles of international law, Mongolia shall:

(a) not view the use of force, or the threat of its use as means of settling any dispute and shall not recognise the results of such use of force or aggression;

(b) not be the first to use its armed forces against another country under any circumstances and pose no military threat to others;

(c) not participate in wars and conflicts unless it falls victim to foreign aggression. It shall fulfill its UN Charter obligations to support UN activities by way of dispatching observers and/or by offering its good offices, mediation and conciliatory services;

(d) not be part of any military alliance unless the independence and sovereignty of Mongolia is directly threatened or there is a clear and present danger of such a threat; and

(e) strictly adhere to the policy of not allowing foreign troops to enter, be stationed in or pass through its territory in the absence of relevant Mongolian legislation. An aspiration to ensure the country's military security by stabilizing the international situation in the Asia-Pacific region is clearly seen in this military doctrine.

Mongolia pledged that it would never engage in a conflict except if invaded and that the country would never enter into any military bloc so long as its independence and sovereignty were not threatened.[10] In sum, the military doctrine has been formulated on the basis of broader security issues particularly in the Asia-Pacific region, and hence the objective of Mongolia's defence policy aims at participating in the creation of collective security systems. Given the fact that Mongolia set its defence objectives on its own, and framed its military doctrine in accordance with the post-Cold War international situation, it can be attributed to the needs imposed by the state and social changes that took place in the early 1990s. On the basis of Mongolia's security strategy, the following paragraphs discuss the issues and concerns related to strategic partnership between Mongolia and Russia during the period of this study.

Mongolia's Status as Nuclear-Weapons-Free Zone

Geographical location and its geopolitical environment make Mongolia extremely sensitive to nuclear issues. During the Cold War, Mongolia as ally of the former Soviet Union hosted Soviet military basis with the primary aim of confronting an emerging nuclear China. About 90 per cent of the weaponry used by the Mongolian military was made in the former Soviet Union.[11] In the late 1960s during Sino-Soviet military stand off, Mongolia risked of becoming involved in possible confrontation between the two nuclear powers. The risk was eliminated only with the normalisation of Sino-Soviet relations and Soviet withdrawal of its troops from Mongolia in 1992. It is to be noted that also nearly 27 per cent of world's nuclear-weapon tests have been conducted in the vicinity of Mongolia the environmental and health consequences of which have yet to be determined.[12] All this made Mongolia, when the Russian basis were withdrawn from the country, to declare its territory a Nuclear-Weapons-Free Zone (NWFZ) in 1992. This was indeed one of the key developments consistent with national interests of Mongolia, through which Mongolia wished to ensure its Nuclear-Weapons-Free Status at the international level and make it an important element of strengthening the country's security by political means.[13] However, the newly adorned status of Mongolia of being a Nuclear-Weapons-Free Zone (NWFZ) was not only targeted to ensure its own security by political means but also to make a contribution to regional stability and predictability. As such the declaration included provisions of banning the deployment and transit of foreign troops, of nuclear weapons and of other weapon of mass destruction on its territory. Later on, it also became a party to the Nuclear non-Proliferation Treaty (NPT) and other relevant international conventions and treaties including Conventions on Destruction of Chemical and Bacteriological Weapons and the Comprehensive Nuclear Weapons Test Ban Treaty (CTBT). On 4th December 1998, the 53rd session of the United Nations General Assembly adopted a resolution 53/77D, entitled "Mongolia's International Security and Nuclear-Weapon-Free Status." Pursuant to paragraph 3 of the resolution, Member States, including the five nuclear-weapon states (P5), were invited to "cooperate with Mongolia in taking the necessary measures to consolidate and strengthen Mongolia's independence, sovereignty and territorial integrity, the inviolability of its borders, its economic security, its ecological balance and its nuclear-weapon-free status as well as its independent foreign policy."[14]

Soni (2002) argues that such an initiative only confirms that Mongolia's security concerns had already been recognised by the world community. On February 3, 2000, a National Law defining and regulating Nuclear-Weapon-Free Status of Mongolia was adopted and passed by the Mongolian Parliament thereby taking a concrete step towards promoting the aims and objectives of nuclear non-proliferation. As a contribution to implementing the UN resolution 53/77D, on October 5, 2000, a joint statement was issued by the P5 countries providing security assurances to Mongolia, which was further transmitted to the UN Security Council.[15] Mongolia, thus, continued to receive assistance and support to promote its international security and nuclear-weapon-free status from various quarters including the relevant UN bodies, the five nuclear-weapon states (P5), the Non Aligned Movement, various regional disarmament meetings etc.[16]

Even in the Ulaanbaatar Declaration issued during Putin's visit to Mongolia in 2000, Russia affirmed "its commitment to the joint declaration by the five nuclear-weapon States [P5] on guarantees for the security of Mongolia in connection with its non-nuclear status. The Mongolian side expressed its appreciation to the Russian side for its efforts to confirm the non-nuclear status of Mongolia and to broaden international recognition thereof." Both Mongolia and Russia supported "the efforts of the countries of Central Asia to create in that region a nuclear-weapon-free zone and consider that, in conjunction with the non-nuclear status of Mongolia, those efforts facilitate the realisation of the goals of strengthening the nuclear non-proliferation regime in the continent of Asia."

Further, on November 20, 2000, the 55th session of the United Nations General Assembly in its another resolution 55/33S on "Mongolia's International Security and Nuclear-Weapon-Free Status" appealed to "the Member States of the Asia and Pacific region to support Mongolia's efforts to join the relevant regional security and economic arrangements."[17] But for the implementing the UN General Assembly Resolution 53/77D, Mongolia required a creative approach that would enable it to "achieve its foreign policy objectives and simultaneously promote regional nuclear security by making Mongolia's policy predictable to its immediate neighbours and other states"[18]. Enkhsaikhan (2006) is of the view that "Mongolia's nuclear-weapon-free policy in its essence is an expression of its rejection of dangerous nuclear policies and of nuclear proliferation, and at the same time a manifestation of its desire for neutrality in nuclear power rivalries or calculations of not only Russia and China but of all nuclear weapon states."[19]

When Mongolia's status as a nuclear-weapon-free zone is fully institutionalised by the conclusion of a trilateral treaty among Russia, Mongolia and China, it would in essence define Mongolia's place and its international role as a source of regional peace, stability and predictability.[20]

It is to be noted that in 1993 itself Russia recognised Mongolia's status as a NWFZ and also agreed to respect the Mongolian policy of not allowing the foreign troops in its territory. [21]

Mongolia-Russia Defence Ties

In the Soviet days in terms of equipment, the Mongolian military remained almost entirely dependent on Soviet arms.[22] However, the Mongolian military's equipment system has already begun to change, and this will inevitably bring about the transformation of its construction, ideas on warfare and even military strategies. Due to its geo-strategic importance, in the post-1991 period, Mongolia became the object of a multinational power struggle between the United States, Russia, China, Japan, Korea, the EU and others. In addition to striving to merge with the West, Mongolia had two possible choices: first, relying once again on its traditional ally, Russia; second, strengthening its strategic links with China. But instead, as discussed in Chapter II, Mongolia pursued a balanced relationship with Russia and China.[23]

Notwithstanding the above facts, shrinking bilateral cooperation between Mongolia and Russia in the defence and military spheres during 1990s caused anxiety in Moscow. Yet, the 1990s also saw at least in the beginning the re-emergence of good neighbourly, equal and mutually beneficial ties between Mongolia and Russia particularly after the signing of the Treaty of Friendly Relations and Cooperation in 1993.[24] The Treaty which was concluded on the basis of equal terms stipulated that Russia would respect Mongolia's policy of denying foreign troops to be stationed or pass through its territory, besides making it clear that neither party would participate in any military or political alliance that would be detriment to the interests of the other. Unlike the 1966 Treaty, the 1993 Treaty was more democratic as although it envisaged wide ranging collaboration, it did not "provide for any form of military alliance and allowed both states to develop relations in accordance with their own national interests." [25]

Simultaneously, Moscow continued to watch with growing nervousness the increasing diversification of Mongolia's military and defence contacts with other countries—China, the United States, South Korea, Japan, India, and Germany.

These contacts have intensified since 1996, especially with the United States. In that year, Ulaanbaatar and Washington signed an agreement on military exchanges and visits that covered diverse areas, including civil-military relations, civil defence, disaster relief, and humanitarian aid. In 1998 and 1999, the two countries conducted a joint civil-defence training exercise, called "Balance Magic." Defence cooperation for military education and training has also grown with the implementation of new programs, costing US $2.5 million per year. [26]

Meanwhile, Russia began taking initiative in restoring relations with Mongolia, and strengthening cooperation in the political and security realms. Moscow's goal was quite clear: to persuade Mongolia to cast off US military influence in order to guarantee both the Siberian region's security and Russia's influence on Central Asian countries. Russia's return to Mongolia is also, to a great extent, due to geo-strategic considerations. With the eastward expansion of the EU and NATO, Russia's strategic space in Central Asia is continuously being nibbled away. If Mongolia falls completely under the influence of the United States or China, the strategic situation for Russia on the Eurasian continent would present a dilemma with no easy solutions.[27]

Overall, in its foreign relations, the defence sector of Mongolia is guided by the basic principles of being multi-pillar, active, equal, and consistent with the national interests as directed by the Government. One of the prominent elements in the centuries-long, comprehensive, and neighborly relationship between Mongolia and Russia was the defence cooperation between them. Presently, defence cooperation between the two sides is based on the "Agreement on military cooperation between the Ministry of Defence of Mongolia and the Ministry of Defence of the Russian Federation" concluded during the visit of the Chief of the General Staff of the Russian Armed Forces to Mongolia in 1993, and on the "Agreement on military and technical cooperation between the Governments of the Russian

Federation and Mongolia" signed during the visit of the Russian Deputy Minister for Foreign Economic Relations of in the same year. These two agreements serve as the legal basis for post-1991 defence relations and cooperation between Mongolia and the Russia.

Though on the ground level nothing concrete could be witnessed in defence ties between Mongolia and Russia during the 1990s, at least the two sides planned several things to carry out. Mongolia, on its part, tried to develop friendly relations in the defence sector with Russia based on the principles of mutual benefit, balance, and consistency with national interests which would contribute to the strengthening of Mongolia's national interests and security in the Asia-Pacific region. Significantly, an official visit to Russia by high-ranking military officials, headed by the Defence Minister of Mongolia in early 1997, was considered as a step towards propelling defence relations between the two neighbors to new heights. During the visit, a considerable amount of work was planned to invigorate defence relations between the two countries and an agreement was reached to conduct cooperation on an annual plan basis. However, no tangible results could be seen in the two countries' defence ties.

Russia had been counting on the weight of economic, military, and cultural factors to ensure that it would remain the leading power in Mongolian affairs. But it remained unsuccessful to achieve that objective, because it lacked the economic wherewithal and remained wedded to a narrow, outdated, geostrategic conception of political influence.[28] Though the visit of Mongolian President N. Bagabandi to Russia in 1999 provided optimism to cooperate on security issues, it was, in fact, in the year 2000 that the issue of bilateral military cooperation was given prominence in the Ulaanbaatar Declaration. The two sides affirmed the importance of reviving cooperation in the military and defence-equipment spheres.

Turning Point in Security Relationship

The visit of the Russian President Vladimir Putin to Mongolia in 2000 turned the tide of Mongolia-Russia security relationship, which was the direct result of an all out effort by both Mongolia and Russia to cooperate in several key areas, including the military one. Putin's visit marked the signing of a 25-point memorandum of cooperation termed as Ulaanbaatar Declaration. It was a document, which determined the principles of directions of extending and developing Mongolia-Russia relations in the 21st century.[29] The declaration displayed that "in many cases both countries see eye to eye on the most important aspects of the global situation, and sets forth the willingness of Moscow and Ulaanbaatar to closely coordinate their policy in international affairs on a wide range of issues".[30] As stated in the Ulaanbaatar Declaration, both Mongolia and Russia expressed their satisfaction at the strengthening of cooperation between the National Security Council of Mongolia and the Security Council of the Russian Federation. They were in favour of continuing their joint efforts and of coordinating their activities in the field of national and international security on the basis of the Protocol on cooperation between the Security Councils of the two countries.

On the issue of strategic partnership, the Ulaanbaatar Declaration provides the following:[31]

(a) Mongolia and Russia emphasised the importance of resuming military and military technical cooperation, and of collaborating in the training of career personnel. Cooperation in those areas will take place in strict accordance with the international obligations of the parties.

(b) The two sides attach great importance to the work, which is in process of completion, of the joint Mongolian-Russian commission on inspection of the State frontier between Mongolia and the Russian Federation with a view to more accurately and clearly marking the frontier line, particularly in areas of intensive economic activity by the frontier populations of the parties.

(c) They will carry out joint and coordinated activities by the law enforcement, frontier and customs bodies and special services of the two countries in order to maintain good order on the Mongolian-Russian frontier, including cooperation to prevent acts of cattle rustling.

Putin's Ulaanbaatar visit also marked the endorsing of a military pact committing to a peaceful future between the two sides.[32] The pact, among other things, also points to develop the impending closer security relationship between Ulaanbaatar and Moscow.[33] Russia, on its part, agreed to provide aid for the training of Mongolian military specialists in addition to launching military cooperation in other areas. At the same time, an agreement to help build a Mongolian nuclear power plant was signed. High officials of the Mongolian National Security Council and their Russian counterparts exchanged visits in April and September 2000, respectively.[34] Anatolii Kwashnin, Chairman of the Russian General Staff, followed up with a visit to Ulaanbaatar in October 2000, the result of which was the signing of documents regarding military cooperation between the Mongolian and Russian armed forces. Bilateral contacts related to border troops and civil defence were also resumed.

Since the issue of bilateral military cooperation was given prominence in the Ulaanbaatar Declaration, the two sides affirmed the importance of reviving cooperation in the military and defence-equipment spheres. Russian General Kwashnin's visit to Mongolia in October 2000 underlined the importance of these matters. Negotiations finally led to agreements to resume the training of Mongolian officers in Russian military colleges and for Russia to assist in repairing and modernizing Russian-made defence equipment, which had long been used by the Mongolian military.[35] In April 2001, Russian Defence Minister Sergei Ivanov declared that Moscow was preparing to help Mongolia upgrade their defence systems and troop training.

In January 2004, when Russia's Minister for Foreign Affairs Igor Ivanov paid an official visit to Mongolia a joint Russia-Mongolia statement was issued in which both sides advocated reinforcing security and cooperation in the Asia-Pacific Region, particularly, in the North East Asia.[36] Both sides also reaffirmed their commitment to the development of multilateral cooperative approaches towards resolution of existing problems in the interest of safeguarding regional stability and security by politico-diplomatic means. It appears that after Putin's visit to Mongolia while the two sides were restoring and developing their conventional bilateral ties in the economic realm, they were also working hard to expand their cooperation in the military field.[37]

What we find from the above facts and analysis is that every state is constrained by circumstances and seeks security and the realisation of national interests within a sea of ever-shifting limitations. A dominant influence on Mongolia's national security is geography and hence its security has, for the past six centuries, been intertwined in its relations with Russia and China and in their relations with one another.[38] After the conclusion of the Cold War, Mongolia abandoned its foreign policy of "leaning" towards the former Soviet Union, and instead established equidistant, friendly relations with both Russia and China, and at the same time, strengthened its relations with the United States, Japan, the EU and other so-called "third neighbours". It thus began pursuing an equidistant, non aligned foreign policy. Since Mongolia is completely encircled by China and Russia, its traffic and communication with the outside world must pass through one of the two counties. If China or Russia refuses to open up airspace or seaports to Mongolia, then its multinational joint exercises with other countries and the successful arrival of the related personnel and equipment would be cut off.

Today, as in the past, only Russia has the potential capability and interests necessary to protect Mongolia from Chinese coercive bullying or military invasion, and only

China is in a position to afford Mongolia similar protection against Russia. Under these conditions, as Magid and Mansbach (1998) argues, that "Mongolia may seek to be one of two in a sphere of three, but the asymmetry in power between Mongolia and either of its potential 'protectors', China or Russia, is so great that the result once again would be to render Mongolia a dependent satellite." However, as Soni (2005) opines that "it is also important to keep in mind that being a land-locked country any future external threat to Mongolia's security by whatever means it is, could be related directly or indirectly with either or both of its two neighbours-Russia and China." Significantly, in 1996, a tripartite border agreement signed in Beijing by Russia, China and Mongolia which defined the western and eastern borders of Mongolia alleviated its concerns about territorial integrity. It was for the first time in the history of relations among the three countries that meeting points of the border lines were demarcated and ratified.[39]

Moreover, the Sino-Soviet rapprochement process resulting from Soviet President Mikhail Gorbachev's Vladivostok proposals witnessed a significant improvement in Mongolia-China relations especially in the 1990s.[40] But the whole idea of changes in Mongolia's security environment which was hitherto affected by the Sino-Soviet row owes much to the withdrawal of Soviet/Russian military forces stationed on the territory of Mongolia.[41] Hence, strategic partnership between Mongolia and Russia has always been based on geostrategic concerns paying much attention to enhance the level of their defence cooperation. Aftermath the visit of Putin to Mongolia Russia has shown keen interest to assist in the modernisation of the Mongolian military without binding to a pro-Russian alignment or treaty, and there are ample signs that military cooperation has been increasing as part of strategic partnership the two countries declared to carry out. On its part, Mongolia would continue, by virtue of its geography, to be of strategic importance to both Russia and China irrespective of the state of their current relations.

Notes and References

1. D. Maygmar (2008), "New Geopolitical Situation and Defence Policy of Mongolia", *The Mongolian Journal of Strategic Studies*, (2): 68.
2. Sharad K. Soni (2002), *Mongolia-Russia Relations: Kiakhta to Vladivostok*, Delhi: Shipra Publications & Maulana Abul Kalam Azad Institute of Asian Studies. 225.
3. See "Concept of National Security of Mongolia", Document, *Strategic Digest*, February 1996, 26 (2): 173.
4. *Ibid.,* p.177.
5. Soni, *Mongolia-Russia Relations*, p. 225.
6. Government of Mongolia (1998), *Mongolian Defence White Paper, 1997-1998,* Ministry of Defence, Ulaanbaatar, p. 38.
7. For the full text of the Law on the Defence of Mongolia, see Government of Mongolia (1995), *Resolution of the State Great Khural, Concept of National Security of Mongolia, Concept of Foreign policy of Mongolia and Fundamentals of Military Doctrine of Mongolia: Documents*, Ulaanbaatar.
8. Government of Mongolia (1998), *Mongolian Defence White Paper, 1997-1998,* Ministry of Defence, Ulaanbaatar, p. 38.
9. *Ibid.,* p. 42.
10. See "The Fundamentals of the Military Doctrine of Mongolia," *Strategic Digest*, 26 (29): 176.
11. Kyodo (2001), "Russia Expresses Willingness to Help Mongolia with Military", 23April, URL: http://findarticles.com/p/articles/mi_m0WDQ/is_2001_April_23/ai_73597758.
12. J. Enkhsaikhan (2000), "Single State NWFZ: From Concept to Practice", *The Mongolian Journal of Strategic Studies*, (2): 19.
13. Soni, *Mongolia-Russia Relations*, p. 226.
14. See United Nations General Assembly (2000), *Report of the Secretary-General on Mongolia's International Security and Nuclear-Weapon-Free Status*, 55th Session, A/55/166, 20th July.

15. See Statement by R. John D. Holum, United States Under Secretary of State for Arms Control and International Security, on behalf of France, the People's Republic of China, the Russian Federation, the United Kingdom of Great Britain and Northern Ireland, and the United States of America, in the United Nations First Committee General Debate, entitled "Security Assurances for Mongolia", 5th October 2000, New York. Also see Appendix IV.
16. *Ibid.*
17. United Nations General Assembly (2001), 55th Session, 69th Plenary Meeting, A/RES/55/33, 12 th January.
18. J. Enkhsaikhan (2000a), "Mongolia's Nuclear-Weapon-Free Status: Concept and Practice", *Asian Survey* (Berkeley), Vol. 40, No. 2, March-April, p. 359; Soni, Sharad K. (2002), *Mongolia-Russia Relations: Kiakhta to Vladivostok*, Delhi: Shipra Publications and Maulana Abul Kalam Azad Institute of Asian Studies.
19. J. Enkhsaikhan (2006), "Mongolia's non-Nuclear Status: An Important Element of North East Asia Security", Paper Presented at the International Conference on *Strengthening the Role of Mongolia in North East Asia*, Ulaanbaatar, 15th February.
20. *Ibid.*
21. G. Tumurchuluun (2001), "Mongolia, Russia and China: The Geopolitical Perspective", *Himalayan and Central Asian Studies*, 5(1): 33-44.
22. Wang Peiran (2009), "Mongolia's Delicate Balancing Act", *China Security*, 5(2): 36.
23. Tumurchuluun, "Mongolia, Russia and China".
24. For full text of the Russo-Mongolian1993 Treaty see, Ministry of Defence of Mongolia (1998), *Mongolian Defence White Paper, 1997-1998*, Ulaanbaatar, pp. 87-92.
25. Galina Yaskina (1998), "Russian-Mongolian Relations: Reality and Outlook", *Far Eastern Affairs*, 5: 37.
26. Porta and Critchfield 2000: 5-6.
27. Wang Peiran (2009), "Mongolia's Delicate Balancing Act", *China Security*, 5(2): 36.

28. Morris Rossabi (2005), *Modern Mongolia: From Khans to Commissars to Capitalists,* Berkeley: University of California Press. p. 204.
29. Soni, *Mongolia-Russia Relations*, p. 227.
30. Leonid Moiseev (2001), "Relations between Russia and Mongolia are Warming", *Far Eastern Affairs*, (1): 12.
31. United Nations General Assembly (2000), *The Ulaanbaatar Declaration issued upon the official visit of Mr. V. V. Putin, President of the Russian Federation on 13 and 14 November 2000 to Mongolia,* A/55/644, 24 November, New York. Also see Appendix III.
32. *Independent* (Dhaka), 15 November 2000, cited in Soni, *Mongolia-Russia Relations,* p. 227.
33. Soni, *Mongolia-Russia Relations*, p.227.
34. Ts. Batbayar (2003), "Mongolian-Russian Relations in the Past Decade," *Asian Survey*, 43(6): p965.
35. *Ibid.*, p968.
36. See *The Joint Russian-Mongolian Statement*, 14th January 2004, URL: http://www.extmin.mn/UBTunhaglaleng.htm
37. BBC News (2001), "Russia-Mongolia Military Deal", April 20, URL: http://news.bbc.co.uk/1/hi/world/europe/1287127.stm
38. Allan M. Wachman (2009), *Mongolia's Geopolitical Gambit: Preserving a Precarious Independence While Resisting "Soft Colonialism",* EAI Fellows Program Working Paper Series 18, Seoul: The East Asia Institute, p. 5.
39. Ministry of External Relations of Mongolia (2000), Mongolian *Foreign Policy Blue Book*, Ulaanbaatar, p. 18.
40. For a detailed description of Gorbachev's Vladivostok initiative, see Soni, *Mongolia-Russia Relations,* pp.217-21.
41. Morris Rossabi (2005), *Modern Mongolia: From Khans to Commissars to Capitalists,* Berkeley: University of California Press. p. 230.

5

Conclusion

The collapse of the former Soviet Union and consequently the communist world brought about the termination of the "cold War" which lasted forty odd years after the end of the Second World War. The termination of the "cold war" implied the end of the division of the world into two parts: the communist world and the free world. However, it did not put an end to other divisions and redivisions of the world, be it interest-based, military, economic, or religious in nature. As redivisions were taking place, realignments too came into fore, thus providing unique opportunities, especially to smaller nations which for centuries have been silent or have been aligned to bigger nations for some reasons or other. Mongolia is one such example of several smaller nations that experienced redivisions and realignments, though in Mongolia's case realignment seems to have been more pronounced as has been discussed in the foregoing chapters taking the case study of Mongolia's relations with Russia during the period between 1991 and 2000.

The conclusions that can be drawn here indicate that Mongolia's realignment with Russia during the period of this study witnessed a marked shift, i.e. based on the principle of equality not on the basis of Russian/Soviet dominance as was the case in the pre-1991 period. In fact, in the post-communist world, Mongolia remained busy in tackling different challenges both internally and externally that gave way to think in terms of improving the conditions in which it operated before. While these developments essentially transformed Mongolia into a political democracy, rapid changes in 1990 and thereafter brought Mongolian society at large face-to-face with a range of serious new problems. Since the scale of economic and societal upheaval has been immense, the structural transition compelled the government to pursue fast-track measures aimed at putting new systems into place. The core issue of national security came into forefront and domestic and foreign policy measures were taken to ensure the political, economic, military and human security. During the Cold War, Mongolia was an "outpost" in the confrontation between the Soviet Union and China, and directly bore the brunt of security pressures from both the north and south. After the Cold War ended Mongolia abandoned its foreign policy of "leaning" towards the Soviet Union, and instead opted for a "multi-pillared" foreign policy. The essence of this policy was striving to form a balance between Russia and China, while at the same time drawing in the United States, Japan, the EU and other "third neighbours" so as to contain Russia and China and guarantee Mongolia's independence and security.

Together with North Korea and Bangladesh, Mongolia ranks among the poorest nations of Asia with per capita income of roughly US $ 600. Yet, its 2.8 million people maintain an adult literacy rate of nearly 99 per cent, making them more literate than the citizens of the much richer United States. High literacy rate indeed helped create an educated Mongolian leadership who could think about their country's future rationally. And there is no doubt that realignment with Russia on quite a new basis, i.e., on the basis of equality in relationship has been a part of this rational thinking. Initially, some politicians and analysts in Moscow suspected the Mongolian leaders of planning to drift farther away from Russia. But later, efforts made by Russian leadership to engage Mongolia by economic means produced encouraging results to strengthen their relationship in political and strategic realms as well which can be gauged through following paragraphs.

Although political relations between Mongolia and Russia in the post-1991 period was affected by ideological factor, encouraging signs emerged when the two sides realised that good neighbourly cooperation between them was necessary to keep away the Chinese from exercising any dominant role in Mongolia. However, despite signing the Declaration of Friendly Relations and Good Neighborly Cooperation in 1991 and the Treaty of Friendly Relations and Good Neighborly Cooperation in 1993, the two sides witnessed a low in their relationship until 2000, when the new Russian President Vladimir Putin's visit to Mongolia was culminated with a joint declaration – the Ulaanbaatar Declaration, which laid a legal groundwork for the restoration of bilateral ties between the two countries. It is to be noted that Putin's visit to Mongolia, which rekindled the hope for Russia and Mongolia to resume and promote their traditional ties, gave a strong push to their so called halted relations and marked the return of Russia's comprehensive cooperation with Mongolia. Ulaanbaatar Declaration indeed saw not only the beginning of a new era in the relationship between the two countries but also helped Russia to try to reestablish its "preeminent position as most favoured neighbor". Since then several high-level bilateral visits took place between the two sides.

As regards the commonality of interests on regional and global issues, Mongolia and Russia made commitments in the Ulaanbaatar Declaration to closely coordinate their efforts on questions of peace, security and cooperation particularly in the Asia-Pacific region. Since both Mongolia and Russia have been increasingly active members of the regional and international community, they have distinction of also being supporters of the Global War on Terror. The two sides remained committed to join forces to oppose international terrorism, religious extremism and national separatism, which threaten regional security, stability and development, and also such forms of criminal activity as illicit trafficking in arms and narcotics and illegal migration. Such commonality of interests on regional and global issues brought the relationship of the two countries in the political field to a new height.

What was revealed in the initial phase of the post-1991 period is that the relationship between the two sides remained dependent on the level of economic stability of each side, as each was going through a bumpy ride in economic development at that time. Economic crisis in Russia naturally weakened its financial and resource supply to Mongolia, which led to rapid deterioration in Mongolia's socio-economic status. Yet in times of relative economic stability, both countries tend to shift their focus to mutually beneficial cooperation without compromising national interests. As regards bilateral economic and trade relations, in the wake of the Soviet collapse in 1991 these were somewhat overshadowed by Mongolia's huge Soviet-era debt to Russia. Roughly three quarters of Mongolia's total debt was spent to fund infrastructure projects.

In an apparent attempt to give bilateral ties a much-needed boost, in December 2003, the Russian government wrote off 98 percent of Mongolia's state debt to Russia, once valued at US $11 billion. However, the move appeared to have a little help to encourage bilateral trade and investment ties. It was hydrocarbon the supplies of which from Russia then became a key factor in reviving economic relations of the two countries. When President Putin visited Mongolia in 2000, an agreement was signed to build an oil pipeline from Siberia to China through Mongolia. Such a project would not only secure lucrative transit fees, but also guarantee stable oil supplies for Mongolia. However, this project, which was delayed due to problems in negotiations among the parties involved, is expected to kick off soon as in Russia's closer ties with Mongolia, energy supplies provide the main leverage over Mongolia.

While in the post-2000 period Russia has been doing much to enhance its position in Mongolia through its efforts to beef up economic cooperation with the Mongolian side, Mongolia too tries to advance its economic growth through Russia's participation in the development of mining resources and infrastructure construction. Mongolian-Russian joint ventures built in early years have all along been the backbone firms in Mongolia, which have created conditions for Russia's future involvement in tapping mine resources and going in for infrastructure development in Mongolia. The petroleum products Mongolia badly needs have all been practically imported from Russia. Notably, Russia has a 49 per cent stake in Mongolia's major copper producer, *Erdenet* and *Mongoltsvetmet* joint ventures. There are more than 250 smaller joint ventures in Mongolia, with combined Russian investments totaling over US $ 20 million. The Russian interest to invest in Mongolia became unprecedented due to the fact that unlike the Soviet period when it was a state investment, in the post-Soviet period it is mainly the interest of Russian businesses with the backing from the Russian Government.

In terms of trade cooperation, particularly since the year 2000 the negative downward trend of the early and mid 1990s has been diminishing and the Russian big business has already begun to turn its eyes to Mongolia. While in 1990, the annual trade turnover between Russia and Mongolia remained at US $ 800 million, it fell in 1994 to US $ 200 million, but in 1995 it again regained to reach at US $ 277 million, which further increased to US $ 319 in 1997 and US $ 396 in 2000, the bulk of which were Russian petrochemical exports. The extent of growing trade between the two sides can be gauged from the fact that within few years in 2006 bilateral trade reached at US$ 592.9 million or nearly 75 per cent up from 2000 figure. Mongolia also remained dependent on Russian spare parts delivery for Mongolian enterprises, in particular for thermo-power stations, all built with Soviet assistance. At a Mongolian-

Russian Intergovernmental Economic Committee meeting held prior to Putin's visit to Mongolia in 2000, the two sides decided that Russia would revise and possibly lower the prices for oil and energy that it exported to Mongolia. Moscow also expressed approval to give more independence concerning trade matters to the Russian regions that border Mongolia, including Buryatia, Kemerovskaya, and Gorno-Altaiskaya.

Strategic Partnership between Mongolia and Russia has been based on geostrategic concerns paying much attention to enhance the level of their defence cooperation. What one could get the impression is that the post-Cold War era has witnessed changes in Mongolia's geopolitical environment and its national security concerns. As stipulated in its *National Security Concept*, Mongolia made commitments to "ensure the security of its existence by strictly observing the policy of not allowing the use of the country's territory against other States; ensuring its Nuclear-Weapons-Free Status at the international level and making it an important element of strengthening the country's security by political means." These commitments led Mongolia in 1992 to declare its territory to be a Nuclear-Weapons-Free Zone (NWFZ) as part of its security policy, and as an essential element of ensuring its non-involvement or neutrality in future Sino-Russian disputes. Moreover, Mongolia's status of being a Nuclear-Weapons-Free Zone was not only targeted to ensure its own security by political means but also to make a contribution to regional stability. As such, the declaration included provisions of banning the deployment and transit of foreign troops, of nuclear weapons and of other weapon of mass destruction on its territory. In such a scenario, developing comprehensive cooperation with Russia became a natural choice for Mongolia in pursuing its national interests.

On its part, Russia has shown keen interest to assist in the modernisation of the Mongolian military without binding to a pro-Russian alignment or treaty, and there are ample signs that military cooperation has been increasing as part of strategic partnership the two countries declared to carry out. Earlier, defence cooperation between the two countries was initiated by concluding two agreements in 1993, i.e., "Agreement on military cooperation between the Ministry of Defence of Mongolia and the Ministry of Defence of the Russian Federation" and "Agreement on military and technical cooperation between the Governments of the Russian Federation and Mongolia." These two agreements serve as the legal basis for defence relations and cooperation between the two sides. Another agreement on defence cooperation was concluded when the Defence Minister of Mongolia visited Russia in 1997. Further, it was in the year 2000 during Putin's visit to Mongolia that a military pact was endorsed committing to a peaceful future between the two sides.

In particular, the issue of bilateral military cooperation was given prominence in the "Ulaanbaatar Declaration". The two sides affirmed the importance of reviving cooperation in the military and defense-equipment spheres. Russian General Kwashnin's visit to Mongolia in October 2000 underlined the importance of these matters. Negotiations led to agreements to resume the training of Mongolian officers in Russian military colleges and for Russia to assist in repairing and modernising Russian-made defense equipment, which had long been used by the Mongolian military.

Notwithstanding the state of relationship with Russia during the period of this study and its aftermath, Mongolia has no choice but to accommodate the political and economic clout of its two neighbours largely due to its being landlocked with a small population and no seaport access of its own. As has long been the case in the past, Mongolia's relations with both the neighbours will continue to have a key impact on its own future. Yet, there are indications from the Mongolian side that they are willing to come even more close to Russia. It is evident from the fact that although Tsakhia Elbegdorj, the current Mongolian President who took over power in

May 2009 is a Democrat, he is considered to be a big supporter of closer ties with Russia. Recently, during an interview with the Russian information agency *Interfax*, he gave strong indications of making changes in Mongolia's external and internal policy which would be oriented more towards developing Mongolia's overall relations with Russia. The idea is that both countries could be able to use their long, friendly relationship to maintain and strengthen peace and stability and create an atmosphere of mutual trust and cooperation in the Asia-Pacific region to extend cooperation and interactions in the areas of politics, economy, and security.

As such the key elements in the growing bilateral relationship between Mongolia and Russia that could affect the ongoing Mongolia-China relations seem to be influenced by, (a) Mongolia's geopolitical relationship with Russia that has always been an important element of Mongolia's security; (b) Mongolia needs Russia for the supply of energy and many other daily commodities, such as sugar and edible oil; and (c) Russia's role as a heavyweight in Eurasia is of great value to Mongolia as it seeks to be connected to Europe. Russia, on the other hand, prefers to have not only a friendly Mongolia but also a Mongolia strategically allied with Russia. For, if Mongolia were to be dominated by China or any other nation, it would represent a dramatic shift in the balance-of-power in the entire region of the Asia-Pacific. As of now, while the Russians see their activities in Mongolia serving as a buffer against a rising China, Mongolians consider it as their geostrategic needs of balancing its relations with the two neighbours.

Due to the mining boom Mongolia has been experiencing today gives her ample scope for further promoting consultations with both Moscow and Beijing on issues ranging from economic and trade to peace and security through strategic partnership. At the same time, Mongolia is also involved in fostering economic interests of other major powers termed as "third neighbours", particularly in the mining field to enhance the country's strategic value and soft power. To sum up, unlike the Soviet period when the determining aspect of Mongolia-Russia relations was ideology, in the post-1991 period it has been the mutual interest which forms the basis of constructive partnership between the two sides in all areas-political, economic and strategic.

Appendices

APPENDIX–I

MONGOLIA-RUSSIA TREATY ON FRIENDLY RELATIONS AND COOPERATION

(20 January 1993)

Mongolia and the Russian Federation (hereinafter referred to as the "Contracting Parties"): proceeding from their traditions of friendly relations, trust, and all-round cooperation, wishing to develop and reinforce an equal and mutually advantageous cooperation between Mongolia and the Russian Federation and, for that purpose, striving to strengthen the legal basis thereof in accordance with the existing situation and development in international relations, confirming their commitment to the objectives and principles of the Charter of the United Nations Organizations, aspiring to contribute to the ensurance of peace and security in the Asia-Pacific region, and to create an atmosphere of mutual understanding and cooperation therein, noting that the Treaty concluded between the People's Government of Mongolia and the Government of the Union of Soviet Socialist Republics in November 5, 1921 played a significant role in the development of good-neighborly relations and cooperation between the two countries, and proceeding from the provisions of the Declaration on friendship and good neighborly cooperation concluded between the MPR and the USSR in February 12, 1991, have agreed as follows:

Article 1

The Contracting Parties will consider themselves as friendly nations and, in their relationship, will be guided by the principle of respect for each other's state sovereignty and independence, of being equally sovereign, of non-use of force, of not threatening with force, of inviolability of state frontiers, of territorial integrity, of non-interference in internal affairs; respect for fundamental human rights and liberties, for equality of rights, for the right to decide destiny on their own; and by the principle of fulfilling in good faith their obligations and cooperating as good neighbors and partners.

Article 2

The Contracting Parties will develop an equal and mutually advantageous cooperation on a sustainable and long-term basis in the political, cultural, arts, educational, scientific and technological, health, defense, ecological, road and transport, telecommunications, information, humanitarian and other fields.

Article 3

The Contracting Parties will consult regularly on deepening their bilateral relations and cooperation, as well as on international issues of mutual interest at various levels. The Contracting Parties will contribute towards developing cooperation between the parliaments and other state bodies of the two countries.

Article 4

The Contracting Parties will not take part in a military and political alliance directed against each other and are obligated not to conclude any treaty or agreement incompatible with the ensurance of the sovereignty and independence of the other Party with a third country. Neither of the Party shall allow a third country to use its territory for an aggression or violence against the other Party. The Russian Federation will respect Mongolia's policy aimed at not allowing stationing and transit passing of foreign troops, nuclear and other weapons of mass destruction on and through its territory.

Article 5

The Contracting Parties will inform each other on possible ways and means of remedying situations that one of the Parties perceives as posing threats to international peace and security and that may bring about disasters of international nature. Following the perception of one of the Parties that its security interests have come under threat, the Contracting Parties will, at the request of the above Party, consult each other.

Article 6

The Contracting Parties will, for the purpose of resolving global- and regional-scale international issues pertaining to the ensurance of peace, security, sustained economic development and environmental protection, strengthen their cooperation within the UN and international organizations.

Article 7

The Contracting Parties will cooperate on a bilateral and multilateral basis so as to render all-round support to the maintenance of stability, the creation of an atmosphere of confidence and

trust, and the promotion of collaboration in the Asia-Pacific region, as well as to the facilitation of contacts among the regional nations in the economic, cultural, humanitarian and other fields.

Article 8

The Contracting Parties will pursue a policy of open economy with each other and develop an equal and mutually advantageous cooperation. For this purpose, they are obligated to mutually provide pleasant conditions for state property and non-state property manufactories, individuals and other legal entities taking part in the commercial, industrial, and financial activities. The Contracting Parties will promote an investment cooperation between themselves or involving a third country partner. The Contracting Parties will provide an all-round support to developing border area trade and cooperation.

Article 9

The Contracting Parties will promote the development of cooperation in the railroad, air transport, authored, and other fields of transportation. The Contracting Parties will also take measures towards enhancing an access capacity of their roadways and improving an organization of transports passing in transit through their territories. Taking into account the fact that Mongolia is landlocked, the Russian Federation will, in accordance with the norms of international law, assist the former in exercising its right to have access to the sea.

Article 10

The Contracting Parties will develop cooperation concerning environmental protection, the ensurance of ecological security, collective prevention from ecological crisis and elimination of the consequences of ecological crisis. For this purpose, the Contracting Parties will, aside from exchanging information on a regular basis, consult on issues directly related to the interests of one of the Parties or either Parties.

Article 11

The Contracting Parties will provide an all-round support to expanding contacts between their citizens. For this purpose, the Contracting Parties will take measures to put in order administrative rules and practices related to mutual transit of their citizens.

Article 12

The Contracting Parties will cooperate on a bilateral and multilateral basis in their combat against organized crime, terrorism, and illegal activities directed at adversely affecting the security of civil air transportation; and against smuggling of arms, drugs, and artworks of cultural and historical value. The Contracting Parties will create conditions necessary for mutual provision of legal assistance in civil, family, and penal proceedings.

Article 13

The Contracting Parties will pay special attention to utilizing achievements of modern technology; cooperating in the field of base and supplementary researches; and creating conditions for implementation of joint programs and projects for the purpose of introducing the results of the above researches to the economy and production.

Article 14

The Contracting Parties will expand and deepen their ties in the fields of culture, arts, science, historical heritage, education, and information. Apart from assisting in the establishment of direct contacts between universities, scientific institutions, and cultural organizations and facilitating an exchange of books, periodicals, cinematographic and theatrical works, and tele- and radio-programs, the Contracting Parties will also encourage mutual study of the languages thereof.

Article 15

So as to implement this Treaty in accordance with the tenets thereof, the Contracting Parties will cooperate towards facilitating direct contacts between aimags of Mongolia and Republics of the Russian Federation, and other administrative and territorial units at all levels, as well as between state, private, and composite property manufactories, offices and organizations.

Article 16

As per the principles of this Treaty, special agreements will be concluded between the Governments of the two Parties and other authorities on herein mentioned and other issues.

Article 17

The Contracting Parties will settle disputed questions that may arise in their relationship by means of goodwill. In case of the impossibility of settling a disputed question by the means as provided for herein, the Contracting Parties will, in accordance with the UN Charter, choose other means of peaceful settling of the disputed question.

Article 18

This Treaty does not affect the Contracting Parties' obligations under effective bilateral and multilateral treaties and agreements concluded by them with other States.

Article 19

This Treaty will remain in force for 20 years and thereafter will be extended every 5 years unless one of the Contracting Parties notifies the other of its intention to terminate the Treaty, in a written form and 12 months before the expiration date of the Treaty's validity.

Article 20

This Treaty requires a process of ratification and enters into force at the time of exchange of ratification documents. This Treaty was done in Moscow on January 20, 1993 in duplicate in the Mongolian and Russian languages, all texts being equally authentic.

For Mongolia	**For The Russian Federation**
P. Ochirbat	**B. Yeltsin**

APPENDIX–II

MONGOLIA-RUSSIA AGREEMENT ON THE AVOIDANCE OF DOUBLE TAXATION WITH RESPECT TO TAXES ON INCOME AND CAPITAL

(5 April 1995)

Article 1

Scope of the Agreement

This Agreement shall apply to persons who, in respect of taxation, are residents of one or both of the Contracting States.

Article 2

Taxes covered

1. This Agreement shall apply to taxes on income and on capital imposed on behalf of a Contracting State, irrespective of the manner in which they are levied.
2. There shall be regarded as taxes on income and on capital all taxes imposed on total income, on total capital, or on elements of income or of capital, including taxes on gains from the alienation of movable or immovable property.
3. The existing taxes to which the Convention shall apply are:

   ...in the case of Mongolia:

   1. the individual income tax;

2. the corporate income tax
(hereinafter referred to as "Mongolian tax");

--in the case of the Russian Federation -- the taxes on income and profits imposed in accordance with the following laws of the Russian Federation:

1. "On the taxes on profits of enterprises and organizations";
2. "On the income tax on individuals"
(hereinafter referred to as "Russian tax").

4. This Agreement shall apply also to any identical or substantially similar taxes on income and on capital which are imposed after the date of signature of this Agreement in addition to, or in place of, the existing taxes. The competent authorities of the Contracting States shall notify each other of any substantial changes which have been made in their respective laws within a reasonable period of time after such changes.

Article 3

General definitions

1. For the purposes of this Agreement, unless the context otherwise requires:

(a) the terms "a Contracting State" and "the other Contracting State" mean Mongolia or Russian Federation as the context requires;

(b) --the term "Mongolia", when used in geographical sense, means all the territory of Mongolia, including air space above it, the area which the tax law of the Contracting State concerned in force, insofar as the State concerned exercises there in conformity with international law sovereign rights to exploit its natural resources;

-- the term "the Russian Federation", when used in geographical sense, means its territory, including internal waters and territorial sea, air space above then as well as economic zone and continental shelf where this State exercises sovereign rights or rights and jurisdiction in conformity with international law and where its tax laws are effective;

(c) the term "person" means an individual, a company and any other body of persons;

(d) the term "company" means any body corporate or any entity which is treated as a body corporate for tax purposes;

(e) the terms "enterprise of a Contracting State" and "enterprise of the other Contracting State" mean respectively an enterprise carried on by a resident of a Contracting State and an enterprise carried on by a resident of the other Contracting State;

(f) the term "nationals" means any individual possessing the citizenship of a Contracting State and all legal persons created under the laws of that Contracting State, as well as, organizations without legal personality treated for tax purposes as legal persons;

(g) the term "international traffic" means any transport by ship, aircraft, road or railway vehicle operated by an enterprise of a Contracting State, except when the ship, aircraft, road or railway vehicle is operated solely between places in the other Contracting State;

(h) the term "competent authority" means:

-- in the case of Mongolia -- the Minister of Finance or his authorized representative;

-- in the case of the Russian Federation -- the Ministry of Finance or its authorized representative.

2. As regards the application of this Agreement by a Contracting State, any term not defined therein shall, unless the context otherwise requires, have the meaning which it has under the laws of that Contracting State concerning the taxes to which this Agreement applies.

Article 4

Resident

1. For the purposes of this Agreement, the term "resident of a Contracting State" means any person who, under the laws of that State, is liable to tax therein by reason of his domicile, residence, place of registration as legal entity or any other criterion of a similar nature.

2. Where by reason of the provisions of paragraph 1, an individual is a resident of both Contracting States, then his status shall be determined as follows:

(a) he shall be deemed to be a resident of the State in which he has a permanent home available to him; if he has a permanent home available to him in both States, he shall be deemed to be a resident of the State with which his personal and economic relations are closer (center of vital interests);

(b) if the State in which he has his center of vital interests cannot be determined, or if he has not a permanent home available to him in either State, he shall be deemed to be a resident of the State in which he has an habitual abode;

(c) if he has an habitual abode in both States or in neither of them, he shall be deemed to be a resident of the State of which he is a national;

(d) if he is a national of both States or of neither of them, the competent authorities of the Contracting States shall settle the question by mutual agreement.

3. Where by reason of the provisions of paragraph 1, a person other than an individual is a resident of both Contracting States, then it shall be deemed to be a resident of the State in which its place of registration of its head office is situated.

Article 5

Permanent Establishment

1. For the purposes of this Agreement, the term "permanent establishment" means a fixed place of activities through which an enterprise of a Contracting State wholly or partly carries out any business in the other Contracting State.
2. The term "permanent establishment" includes especially:
   (a) a place of management;
   (b) a branch;

(c) an office;

(d) a factory;

(e) a workshop;

(f) a mine, an oil or gas well, a quarry or any other place of extraction of natural resources;

(g) a building site or construction, assembly or installation project or supervisory activities, in connection therewith, constitute a permanent establishment but only if such site, project or activities lasts more than 24 months.

3. Notwithstanding the preceding provisions of this Article the term "permanent establishment" shall be deemed not to include:

(a) the use of facilities solely for the purpose of storage, display or delivery of goods or merchandise belonging to the enterprise;

(b) the maintenance of a stock of goods or merchandise belonging to the enterprise solely for the purpose of storage, display or delivery;

(c) the maintenance of a stock of goods or merchandise belonging to the enterprise solely for the purpose of processing by another enterprise;

(d) the maintenance of a fixed place of business solely for the purpose of purchasing goods or merchandise or of collecting information for the enterprise;

(e) the maintenance of a fixed place of business solely for the purpose of carrying on for the enterprise any other activity of a preparatory or auxiliary character;

(f) the maintenance of a fixed place of business solely for any combination of activities mentioned in subpara graphs (a) to (e), provided that the overall activity of the fixed place of business resulting from this combination is of preparatory or auxiliary character.

4. Notwithstanding the provisions of paragraphs 1 and 2, where a person -- other than an agent of independent status to whom the provisions of paragraph 5 apply -- is acting on behalf of an enterprise and has and habitually exercises in the Contracting State an authority to conclude contracts in the name of the enterprise, that

enterprise shall be deemed to have a permanent establishment in that Contracting State in respect of any activities which that person undertakes for the enterprise, unless the activities of such person are limited to those mentioned in paragraph 3 which, if exercised though a fixed place of business would not make this fixed place of business a permanent establishment under the provisions of that paragraph.

5. An enterprise of a Contracting State shall not be deemed to have a permanent establishment in the other Contracting State merely because it carries on business in that other State through a broker, general commission agent or any other agent of an independent status, provided that such persons are acting in the ordinary course of their business. However, when the activities of such an agent are devoted wholly or almost wholly on behalf of that enterprise, he will not be considered an agent of an independent status within the meaning of this paragraph.
6. The fact that a company which is a resident of a Contracting State controls or is controlled by a company which is a resident of the other Contracting State, or which carries on business in that other State (whether through a permanent establishment or otherwise), shall not of itself constitute either company a permanent establishment of the other.

Article 6

Income from immovable property

1. Income derived by a resident of a Contracting State from immovable property (including income from agriculture or forestry) situated in the other Contracting State may be taxed in that other Contracting State.
2. The term "immovable property" shall have the meaning which it has under the law of the Contracting State in which the property in question is situated. The term shall in any case include property accessory to immovable property, livestock and equipment used in agriculture

and forestry or fishing place of every kind, rights to which the provisions of general law respecting landed property apply, usufruct of immovable property and rights to variable or fixed payments as consideration for the working of, or the right to work mineral deposits, sources and other natural resources. Ships, aircraft, road and railway vehicles shall not be regarded as immovable property.

3. The provisions of paragraph 1 shall apply to income derived from the direct use, letting, or use in any other form of immovable property.
4. The provisions of paragraphs 1 and 3 shall also apply to the income from immovable property of an enterprise and to income from immovable property used for performance of independent personal services.

Article 7

Business profits

1. The profits derived in a Contracting State by an enterprise of the other Contracting State may be taxed in the first-mentioned State only if it is derived through a permanent establishment situated therein and only so much of them as is attributable to the activity of such permanent establishment.
2. Subject to the provisions of paragraph 3, where an enterprise of a Contracting State carries on business in the other Contracting State through a permanent establishment situated therein, there shall in each Contracting State be attributed to that permanent establishment the profits which it might be expected to make if it were a distinct and separate enterprise engaged in the same or similar activities under the same or similar conditions and dealing wholly independently with the enterprise of which it is a permanent establishment.
3. In determining the profits of a permanent establishment, there shall be allowed as deductions expenses which are incurred for the purposes of the business of the permanent

establishment, including executive and general administrative expenses so incurred, whether in the State in which the permanent establishment is situated or elsewhere.

4. No profits shall be attributed to a permanent establishment by reason of the mere purchase by that permanent establishment of goods or merchandise for the enterprise.
5. Where profits include items of income which are dealt with separately in other Articles of this Agreement, then the provisions of those Articles shall not be affected by the provisions of this Article.

Article 8

Shipping, air, road and railway transport

1. Profits of an enterprise of a Contracting State derived from the other Contracting State from the operation of ships, aircraft or road and railway vehicle in international traffic shall be taxable only in the Contracting State in which a place of registration of head-office of this enterprise is situated.
2. For the purpose of this Agreement, profits (or income) from international traffic shall include profits (or income) from the direct use, profits (or income) from the lease or use in any other form of means of transportation, mentioned in paragraph 1 of this Article, including profits (or income) from the use, maintenance and lease of containers and other related equipment.
3. If the place of effective management of a shipping enterprise is aboard a ship, then it shall be deemed to be situated in the Contracting State in which the home harbor of the ship is situated; or, if there is no such home harbor, in the Contracting State of which the operator of the ship is a resident.
4. The provisions of paragraph 1 and 2 shall also apply to income from the participation in a pool, a joint-business, or an international operating agency.

Article 9

Possible adjustments to income

1. Where

(a) an enterprise of a Contracting State participates directly or indirectly in the management, control or capital of an enterprise of the other Contracting State, or

(b) the same persons participate directly or indirectly in the management, control or capital of an enterprise of a Contracting State and an enterprise of the other Contracting State,

and in either case conditions are made or imposed between the two enterprises in their commercial or financial relations which differ from those which would be made between independent enterprises, then any profits which would, but for those conditions, have accrued to one of the enterprises, but, by reason of those conditions, have not so accrued, may be included in the profits of that enterprise and taxed accordingly.

2. Where a Contracting State includes in the profits of an enterprise of that State -- and taxes accordingly -- profits on which an enterprise of the other Contracting State has been charged to tax in that other State and the profits so included are by the first-mentioned State claimed to be profits which would have accrued to that enterprise of the first-mentioned State if the conditions made between the two enterprises have been those which would have been made between independent enterprises, then that other State shall make an appropriate adjustment to the amount of the tax charged therein on those profits, where that other State considers the adjustment justified. In determining such adjustments due regard shall be had to the other provisions of this Agreement and the competent authorities of the Contracting States shall, if necessary, consult each other.

Article 10

Dividends

1. Dividends paid by a company which is a resident of a Contracting State to a resident of the other Contracting State may be taxed in that other State.
2. However, such dividends may also be taxed in the Contracting State of which the company paying the dividends is a resident and according to the laws of that State, but if the recipient is the beneficial owner of the dividends the tax so charged shall not exceed 10 per cent of the gross amount of the dividends.
3. The term "dividends" as used in this Article means income from share, or other rights, not being debt-claims, participating in profits, as well as income from other corporate rights which is subject to the same taxation treatment as income from shares by the laws of the State of which the company making the distribution is a resident.
4. The provisions of paragraph 1 and 2 shall not apply if the beneficial owner of the dividends, being a resident of a Contracting State, carries on or carried on business in the other Contracting State of which the company paying the dividends is a resident, through a permanent establishment, or performs independent personal services from a fixed base situated therein and the dividends are attributable to such permanent establishment or fixed base. In such case the provisions of Article 7 or 14 of this Agreement, as the case may be, shall apply.

Article 11

Interest

1. Interest arising in a Contracting State and paid to a resident of the other Contracting State may be taxed in that other State.
2. However, such interest may also be taxed in the Contracting State in which it arises and according to the

laws of that State, but if the recipient is the beneficial owner of interest, the tax so charged shall not exceed 10 per cent of the gross amount of the interest.

3. Notwithstanding the provisions of paragraph 2, interest arising in:

-- Mongolia and paid to the Government of the Russian Federation or to the Central Bank of the Russian Federation or to the Foreign Trade Bank of the Russian Federation shall be exempt from the Mongolian tax;

-- the Russian Federation and paid to the Government of Mongolia or to the Central Bank of Mongolia (Mongol Bank) or to the Trade and Development bank of Mongolia shall be exempt from the Russian tax.

4. The term "interest" as used in this Article means income from debt-claims of every kind, whether or not secured by mortgage and whether or not carrying a right to participate in the debtor's profits, and in particular, income from government securities and income from bonds and debentures, including premiums and prizes attaching to such securities, bonds or debentures.

5. The provisions of paragraphs 1 and 2 and 3 shall not apply if the beneficial owner of the interest, being a resident of a Contracting State, carries on or carried on business in the other Contracting State in which the interest arises, through a permanent establishment, or performs independent personal services from a fixed base situated therein, and the debt-claim in respect of which the interest is paid is effectively connected with such permanent establishment or fixed base. In such case the provisions of Article 7 or Article 14 of this Agreement, as the case may be, shall apply.

6. Interest shall be deemed to arise in a Contracting State when the payer is the Government of that State, a local authority or a resident of that State. Where, however, the person paying the interest, whether he is a resident of a Contracting State or not, has in a Contracting State a permanent establishment or fixed base in connection with which the indebtedness on which the interest is paid was incurred, and such interest is borne by such

permanent establishment or fixed base, then such interest shall be deemed to arise in the State in which the permanent establishment of fixed base is situated.

7. Where, by reason of a special relationship between the payer and the beneficial owner or between both of them and some other person, the amount of the interest, having regard to the debt-claim for which it is paid, exceeds the amount which would have been agreed upon by the payer and the beneficial owner in the absence of such relationship, the provisions of this Article shall apply only to the last-mentioned amount. In such case, the excess part of the payments shall remain taxable according to the laws of each Contracting State, due regard being had to the other provisions of this Agreement.

Article 12

Royalties

1. Royalties arising in a Contracting State and paid to a resident of the other Contracting State may be taxed in that other State.
2. However, such royalties may also be taxed in the Contracting State in which they arise and according to the laws of that State.
3. The term "royalties" as used in this Article means payments of any kind received as a consideration for the use of, of the right to use, any copyright of literary, artistic or scientific work including cinematograph films and films or tapes used for radio or television broadcasting, any patent, know-how, trade mark, design or model, plan, secret formula or process, or for the use of, or the right to use industrial, commercial or scientific equipment, or for information concerning industrial, commercial or scientific experience.
4. The provisions of paragraphs 1 and 2 shall not apply if the beneficial owner of the royalties, being a resident of a Contracting State, carries on business in the other Contracting State in which the royalties arise, through a permanent establishment situated therein, or performs

in that other State independent personal services through a fixed base situated therein and the right or property in respect of which the royalties are paid is effectively connected with such permanent establishment or fixed base. In such case the provisions of Articles 7 and 14, as the case may be, shall apply.

5. Royalties shall be deemed to arise in a Contracting State when the payer is the Government of that State, a local authority or a resident of that State. Where, however, the person paying the royalties, whether he is a resident of a Contracting State or not, has in a Contracting State a permanent establishment or a fixed base in connection with which the liability to pay the royalties was incurred, and such royalties are borne by such permanent establishment or fixed base, then such royalties shall be deemed to arise in the State in which the permanent establishment or fixed base is situated.

6. Where, by reason of a special relationship between the payer and the beneficial owner or between both of them and some other person, the amount of the royalties paid, having regard to the use, right or information for which they are paid, exceeds the amount which would have been agreed upon by the payer and the beneficial owner in the absence of such relationship, the provisions of this Article shall apply only to the last-mentioned amount. In such case, the excess part of the payments shall remain taxable according to the laws of each Contracting State, due regard being had to the other provisions of this Agreement. .

Article 13

Capital gains

1. Gains derived by a resident of a Contracting State from the alienation of immovable property referred to in Article 6 and situated in the other Contracting State may be taxed in that other State.
2. Gains derived from the alienation of movable property forming part of a permanent establishment which an

enterprise of a Contracting State has in the other Contracting State, or of movable property pertaining to a fixed base available to a resident of a Contracting State in the other Contracting State for the purpose of performing independent personal services, including such gains from the alienation of such a permanent establishment or of such a fixed base, may be taxed in that other State.

The term "movable property" means property which is recognized as such by the legislation of the Contracting State where such property is located.

3. Gains derived by a resident of a Contracting State from the alienation of ships, aircraft, road and railway vehicles operated in international traffic or movable property pertaining to the operation of such ships, aircraft, road and railway vehicles shall be taxable only in the Contracting State of which the alienator is a resident.
4. Gains derived from the alienation of any property such as shares in a company or securities, bonds, debentures and alike shall be taxable only in the Contracting State of which the alienator is a resident.

Article 14

Independent personal services

1. Income derived by an individual who is a resident of a Contracting State from the performance of professional services or other activities of an independent character shall be taxable only in that State, unless such services are performed or were performed in the other Contracting State and the income attributable to a fixed base which the individual has or had regularly available to him in that other State.
2. The term "professional services" includes especially independent scientific, literary, artistic, educational or teaching activities, as well as the independent activities of physicians, lawyers, engineers, architects, dentists and accountants.

Article 15

Dependent personal services

1. Subject to the provisions of Articles 16, 18 and 19, salaries, wages and other similar remuneration derived by a resident of a Contracting State in respect of an employment shall be taxable only in that Contracting State unless the employment is exercised in the other Contracting State. If the employment is so exercised, such remuneration as is derived therefrom may be taxed in that other Contracting State.
2. Notwithstanding the provisions of paragraph 1, remuneration derived by a resident of a Contracting State in respect of an employment exercised in the other State shall be taxable only in the first-mentioned State, if:
   (a) the recipient is present in the other Contracting State for a period or periods not exceeding in the aggregate 183 days in the calendar year concerned; and
   (b) the remuneration is paid by, or on behalf of, an employer who is not a resident of the other Contracting State; and
   (c) the remuneration is not borne by a permanent establishment or fixed base which the employer has in the other State.
3. Notwithstanding the provisions of paragraphs 1 and 2, salaries and other remuneration derived by the resident of a Contracting State for work carried out in the other Contracting State are not taxed in that other State if it is performed by persons:
   (a) in respect of an employment exercised aboard a ship, aircraft or road and railway vehicle operated in international traffic by an enterprise of a Contracting State in which the place of registration of head-office of this enterprise is situated;
   (b) in respect of remuneration derived as a journalist or a correspondent provided that such payment is made

from sources of the State in which he is a resident for a period of five years from the date of his arrival to the other Contracting State.

Article 16

Directors' fees

Directors' fees and other similar payments derived by a resident of a Contracting State in his capacity as a member of the Board of Directors of a company which is a resident of the other Contracting State may be taxed in that other State.

Article 17

Entertainers and Sportsmen

1. Notwithstanding the provisions of Articles 14 and 15, income derived by a resident of a Contracting State as an entertainer, such as a theatre, motion picture, radio or television artists, or a musician, or as a sportsman, from his personal activities as such exercised in the other Contracting State, may be taxed in that other State.
2. Where income in respect of personal activities exercised by an entertainer or a sportsman in his capacity as such accrues not to the entertainer or sportsman himself but to another person, that income may, notwithstanding the provisions of Articles 7, 14 and 15, be taxed in the Contracting State in which the activities of the entertainer or sportsman are exercised.
3. Notwithstanding the provisions of paragraphs 1 and 2, income derived by entertainers or sportsmen who are residents of a Contracting State shall be exempt from tax in the other Contracting State if the visit to that State is supported by the Government of the other State, administrative-territorial subdivision or a local authority thereof.

Article 18

Pensions

Subject to the provisions of paragraph 2 of Article 19, pension and other similar remuneration paid to a resident of a Contracting State in consideration of past employment shall be taxable only in that Contracting State.

Article 19

Government Services

(a) Remuneration, other than a pension, paid by a Government of a Contracting State, administrative-territorial subdivision or local authority thereof to any individual in respect of services rendered to the Government of that State, administrative-territorial subdivision or local authorities thereof shall be taxable only in that State.

(b) However, such remuneration shall be taxable only in the other Contracting State if the services are rendered in that other Contracting State and the recipient is a resident of that State who:

1. is a national of that other State not being a national of the first-mentioned State; or
2. not being a national of the first-mentioned State did not become a resident of that State solely for the purpose of rendering the services.

2. (a) Any pension paid by, or out of funds to which contributions are made by the Government of a Contracting State, administrative-territorial subdivision or local authority thereof to an individual in respect of services rendered to the Government of that State, administrative- territorial subdivision or local authority shall be taxable only in that State.

(b) However, such pension shall be taxable only in the other Contracting State if the individual is a resident and a national of that other State.

3. The provisions of paragraphs 1 and 2 of this Article shall not apply and the provisions of Articles 15, 16, 17 and 18 shall apply to remuneration and pensions paid by a Contracting State, administrative-territorial subdivision or local authority thereof if such remuneration or pensions are paid in respect of services rendered in connection with any business activities carried on in the Contracting State.

Article 20

Teachers and researchers

An individual who is or immediately before visiting a Contracting State was a resident of the other Contracting State and is present in the first-mentioned Contracting State for the primary purpose of teaching, giving lectures or conducting research at a university, college, school or other educational institution or scientific research institution on an official invitation of above-indicated organizations shall be exempt from tax in the first-mentioned Contracting State for a period of three years from the date of his first arrival in the first-mentioned Contracting State, in respect of remuneration for such teaching, lecture or research.

Article 21

Students and business apprentices

A student or business apprentice who is or was immediately before visiting a Contracting State a resident of the other State and who is present in the first-mentioned State solely for the purpose of his education or training shall not be taxed in that first-mentioned State on the following payments or income received or derived by him for the purpose of his maintenance, education or training:

(a) payments derived from sources outside that Contracting State;

(b) scholarships or awards supplied by the Government, or by a scientific, educational, cultural or other non-profit organization of a Contracting State.

Article 22

Other income

1. Items of income of a resident of a Contracting State, wherever arising, not dealt with in the foregoing Articles of this Agreement shall be taxable only in that Contracting State.
2. The provisions of paragraph 1 shall not apply to income other than income from immovable property as defined in paragraph 2 of Article 6, if the recipient of such income, being a resident of a Contracting State, carries on business in the other Contracting State through a permanent establishment situated therein, or performs in that other State independent personal services from a fixed base situated therein, and the right and property in respect of which the income is paid is effectively connected with such permanent establishment or fixed base. In such case the provisions of Article 7 or Article 14, as the case may be, shall apply.

Article 23

Taxation of capital

1. Capital represented by immovable property, as defined in Article 6, owned by a resident of a Contracting State may be taxed in the Contracting State in which such property is situated.
2. Capital represented by movable property forming part of the business property of a permanent establishment which an enterprise of a Contracting State has in the other Contracting State or by movable property pertaining

to a fixed base available to a resident of a Contracting State in the other Contracting State for the purpose of performing independent personal services, may be taxed in that other State.

3. Capital represented by ships, aircraft, road and railway vehicles operated in international traffic or by movable property pertaining to the operations of such means of transport shall be taxable only in the Contracting State where a possessor of this capital is a resident.

4. All other elements of capital of a resident of a Contracting State shall be taxable only in that State in which the capital is located.

Article 24

Elimination of double Taxation

-- In Mongolia double taxation shall be eliminated as follows:

(a) Where a resident of Mongolia derives from the Russian Federation, the amount of tax that is payable in the Russian Federation in accordance with the provisions of this Agreement may be credited against the Mongolian tax imposed on that resident. The amount of the credit, however, shall not exceed the amount of the Mongolian tax on that income computed in accordance with the taxation laws and regulations of Mongolia.

(b) The profits of non-residents of a Contracting State derived from the other Contracting State, shall not be attributed to taxation in the first-mentioned Contracting State.

(c) Notwithstanding the provisions of sub-paragraph (a), if one of the Contracting States exempts its residents with respect to income derived from the other Contracting State in the form of dividends, interest and royalties from taxation in accordance with its national tax legislation, the other Contracting State in its turn also exempts this income from taxation in accordance with its national legislation. This provision in any case shall prevail over the provisions of paragraph 2 of Article 10, paragraph 2 of Article 11 and of Article 12.

-- In the Russian Federation double taxation shall be eliminated as follows:

(a) Where a resident on the Russian Federation derives income from Mongolia, the amount of tax that is payable in Mongolia in accordance with the provisions of this Agreement, may be credited against the tax levied in the Russian Federation. The amount of credit, however, shall not exceed the amount of the Russian Federation tax on that income computed in accordance with the taxation laws and regulations of the Russian Federation.

(b) The profits of non-residents of a Contracting State derived from the other contracting State, shall not be attributed to taxation in the first-mentioned Contracting State.

(c) Notwithstanding the provisions of sub-paragraph (a) if one of the Contracting States exempts its residents with respect to income derived from the other Contracting State in the form of dividends, interest and royalties from taxation in accordance with its national tax legislation, the other Contracting State in its turn also exempts this income from taxation in accordance with its national legislation. This provision in any case shall prevail of the provisions of paragraph 2 of Article 10, paragraph 2 of Article 11 and of Article 12.

Article 25

Non-discrimination

1. Nationals of a Contracting State shall not be subjected in the other Contracting State to any taxation or any requirement connected therewith, which is other or more burdensome than the taxation and connected requirements to which nationals of that other State in the same circumstances are or may be subjected. This provision shall, notwithstanding the provisions of Article 1, also apply to persons who are not residents of one or both of the Contracting States.

2. The taxation on a permanent establishment which an enterprise of a Contracting State has in the other Contracting State shall not be less favourably levied in that other State than the taxation levied on the enterprise of that other State carrying on the same activities. This provision shall not be construed as obliging a Contracting State to grant to residents of the other Contracting State any personal allowances, reliefs and reductions for taxation purposes on account of civil status or family responsibilities which it grants to its own residents.
3. Except where the provisions of paragraph 1 of Article 9, paragraph 6 of Article 11, or paragraph 6 of Article 12 apply, interest, royalties and other disbursements paid by an enterprise of a Contracting State to a resident of the other Contracting State shall, for the purpose of determining the taxable profits of such enterprise, be deductible under the same conditions as if they had been paid to a resident of the first-mentioned State.
4. Enterprises of a Contracting State, the capital of which is wholly or partly owned or controlled, directly or indirectly, by one or more residents of the other Contracting State, shall not be subjected in the first-mentioned State to any taxation or any requirement connected therewith which is other or more burdensome than the taxation and connected requirements to which other similar enterprises of the first-mentioned State are or may be subjected.
5. The provisions of this Article shall, notwithstanding the provisions of Article 2, apply to taxes of every kind and description.

Article 26

Mutual agreement procedure

1. Where a person considers that the actions of one or both of the Contracting States result or will result for him in taxation not in accordance with the provisions of this Agreement, he may, irrespective of the remedies provided by the domestic law of those States, present his case to

the competent authority of the Contracting State of which he is a resident or, if his case comes under paragraph 1 of Article 25, to that of the Contracting State of which he is a national. The case must be presented within three years from the first notification of the action resulting in taxation not in accordance with the provisions of the Agreement.

2. The competent authority shall endeavour, if the objection appears to it to be justified and if it is not itself able to arrive at a satisfactory solution, to resolve the case by mutual agreement with the competent authority of the other Contracting State, with a view to the avoidance of taxation which is not in accordance with the provisions of this Agreement.
3. The competent authorities of the Contracting States shall endeavour to resolve by mutual agreement any difficulties or doubts arising as to the interpretation or application of the Agreement. They may also consult together for the elimination of double taxation in cases not provided for in this Agreement.
4. The competent authorities of the Contracting States may communicate with each other directly for the purpose of reaching an agreement in the sense of the preceding paragraphs. When it seems advisable for reaching agreement, representatives of the competent authorities of the Contracting State may meet together for an oral exchange of opinions.

Article 27

Exchange of information

1. The competent authorities of the Contracting State shall exchange such information as is necessary for carrying out the provisions of this Agreement or of the domestic laws of the Contracting States concerning taxes covered by the Agreement insofar as the taxation thereunder is not contrary to the Agreement. Any information received by a Contracting State shall be treated as confidential in the same manner as information obtained under the

domestic laws of that State and shall be disclosed only to persons or authorities (including courts and administrative bodies) involved in the assessment or collection of, the enforcement or prosecution to, the taxes covered by the Agreement. Such persons or authorities shall use the information only for such purposes. They may disclose the information in public court proceedings or in judicial decisions.

2. In no case shall the provisions of paragraph 1 be construed so as to impose on a Contracting State the obligation:
   (a) to carry out administrative measures at variance with the laws and administrative practice of that or of the other Contracting State;
   (b) to supply information which is not obtainable under the laws or in the normal course of the administration of that or of the other Contracting State;
   (c) to supply information which would disclose any trade, business, industrial, commercial or professional secret or trade process, or information, the disclosure of which would be contrary to public policy (public order).

Article 28

Employees of diplomatic and consular establishments

Nothing in this Agreement shall affect the fiscal privileges of the employees of diplomatic and consular establishments under the general rules of international law or under the provisions of special agreements.

Article 29

Entry into force

1. This Agreement shall be subject to ratification in each Contracting State.
2. This Agreement shall enter into force on the date of exchange of instruments of ratification and its provisions shall have effect:

(a) in respect of tax withheld at source, for amounts paid or credited on or after the first day of January in the calendar year, following the year in which the Agreement enters into force;

(b) in respect of other income taxes, for the taxable period beginning on or after the first day of January in the calendar year, following the year in which the Agreement enters into force.

3. Since the entry into effect of this Agreement, the application of the Multilateral Convention for the avoidance of double taxation with respect to income and capital of individuals signed in Miscolc on 27 May 1977 and the Multilateral Convention for the avoidance of double taxation with respect to income and capital of legal persons signed in Ulan-Bator on 19 May 1978 shall, in relations between Mongolia and the Russian Federation, cease to have effect.

4. If any tax provision of an Agreement signed or concluded between the Contracting States is more favourable for taxpayers than the similar tax provision which this Agreement contains, the provision which is more favourable may apply.

Article 30

Termination

The Agreement shall remain in force indefinitely, but either of the Contracting States may on or before the thirtieth day of June in any calendar year from the fifth year following that in which the instruments of ratification have been exchanged, give written notice of termination to the other Contracting State through diplomatic channels. In such event this Agreement shall cease to have effect:

(a) in respect of tax withheld at source, for amounts paid or credited on or after the first day of January in the calendar year next following that in which the notice is given; and

(b) in respect of other income taxes, for the taxable period beginning on or after the first day of January in the calendar year next that in which the notice is given.

Done in duplicate, this fifth day of April 1995, in Moscow, each in Mongolian, Russian and English languages, all three texts being equally authentic. In case of divergence between the texts, the English text shall be the operative one.

APPENDIX–III

MONGOLIA-RUSSIA ULAANBAATAR DECLARATION

(14 November 2000)

At the invitation of Mr. Natsagiin Bagabandi, President of Mongolia, the President of the Russian Federation, Mr. Vladimir Putin, made an official visit to Mongolia on 13 and 14 November 2000.The leaders of the two States held a thorough exchange of views on a broad range of questions concerning their bilateral relations and on international issues of mutual interest. The meetings and talks held in Ulaanbaatar between the leaders of Mongolia and the Russian Federation constitute an important stage in the development of the traditionally friendly relations between the two countries.

1. Mongolia and the Russian Federation reaffirm their commitment to the Treaty of Friendship and Cooperation between Mongolia and the Russian Federation of 20 January 1993. They share an understanding that Mongolian-Russian cooperation in various areas in the new century must move forward in accordance with the provisions of the Charter of the United Nations and the norms of international law and equity, the principles of respect for sovereignty, equality of rights, mutual advantage and territorial integrity, and also on the basis of the traditions of friendship and good-neighbourliness built up over many decades. Convinced of the need to build a multipolar structure for peace, and underscoring the special importance of the development of inter-State

relations in Asia, without division into blocs, the parties reaffirm that they will not participate in any military-political unions directed against each other, and undertake not to conclude with third countries any treaties or agreements which are incompatible with the interests of the sovereignty and independence of the other party. Neither party will allow its territory to be used by a third State for the purposes of aggression or any other act of force prejudicial to the sovereignty, security and public order of the other party.

2. The parties attach importance to the holding of regular meetings at the senior and high levels in the future and to cooperation between their government bodies, including within the framework of the Mongolian-Russian Intergovernmental Commission on Economic, Trade, Scientific and Technical Cooperation.
3. The parties welcome the development of regional and border contacts and will make efforts to develop the legal basis for further expanding and deepening them. The Mongolian side is interested in active cooperation with the regional structures of the Russian Federation, including the interregional association "Siberian Accord".
4. Noting that there exists significant potential for increased economic and trade cooperation, the Presidents of Mongolia and the Russian Federation instructed the respective organs of the executive authorities in their countries to consider, in a constructive spirit, questions relating to the liberalization and expansion of reciprocal trade, including the establishment of favourable railway rates, customs duties and other charges, within the framework of the negotiations begun on these questions, with a view to completing them in 2001.
5. Considering economic cooperation with each other as an integral part of the regional cooperation being established in North-East Asia, Ulaanbaatar and Moscow attach great significance to the large-scale energy projects envisaged for the region in the twenty-first century - the installation of major gas and oil pipelines and power transmission lines. The Russian side is in favour of

Mongolia's participation in such projects, taking into account the economic and geographic factors. The parties regard cooperation among the States members of the Economic and Social Commission for Asia and the Pacific (ESCAP) in the field of transport as a very important trend and, in this connection, invite all the parties concerned to make use of the Mongolian railway system and the Trans-Siberian railroad with a view to optimizing transport routes between Europe and the Asia-Pacific region. The parties agreed to continue the trilateral expert consultations for the conclusion of a basic (framework) agreement on through carriage between Mongolia, the Russian Federation and the People's Republic of China, understanding, in this regard, the need to improve existing mechanisms in the field of through carriage at the national, bilateral and international levels.

6. The parties expressed their support for increasing the efficiency of and modernizing the major Mongolian-Russian joint enterprises - "Erdenet", "Mongolrostzvetmet" and "UBZHD", which constitute a vitally important part of the Mongolian economy. They also agreed to make every effort to encourage mutual investments through the creation of new joint enterprises on the basis of various forms of ownership, and also through the participation of business enterprises of the two countries in privatization projects in Mongolia and the Russian Federation. The parties deemed it appropriate to formulate a programme for the development of cooperation in the industrial field and resume mutually advantageous cooperation in developing Mongolian agricultural production.
7. The parties considered questions involving cooperation in the supply of Russian energy sources to Mongolia, taking into account the need to ensure its stability on the basis of yearly protocols on economic and trade cooperation.
8. Nature conservation and environmental security constitute an important area of cooperation between the

two countries in the context of current global development. The parties will collaborate actively to prevent forest and steppe fires, natural disasters and potential technological catastrophes.

9. Mongolia and the Russian Federation are committed to preserving and strengthening the traditionally close spiritual and cultural ties between the peoples of the two countries. They will encourage contacts between people and between social, scientific, sport and youth organizations of the two countries. The Russian side will continue to provide assistance in the training of Mongolian national personnel in Russian higher educational establishments. The parties will support cooperation in the study of the Mongolian and Russian languages and of each other's historical and cultural heritage.
10. The parties agreed to entrust the appropriate ministries and departments with the task of further studying aspects of the liberalization of conditions for reciprocal travel by citizens, improving arrangements for issuing them with visas and extending the range of persons to whom visas are issued without charge or for substantially lower fees.
11. Expressing their satisfaction at the strengthening of cooperation between the National Security Council of Mongolia and the Security Council of the Russian Federation, the parties were in favour of continuing their joint efforts and of coordinating their activities in the field of national and international security on the basis of the Protocol on cooperation between the Security Councils of the two countries.
12. The parties emphasized the importance of resuming military and military technical cooperation, and of collaborating in the training of career personnel. Cooperation in those areas will take place in strict accordance with the international obligations of the parties.
13. Mongolia and the Russian Federation attach great importance to the work, which is in process of completion, of the joint Mongolian-Russian commission on inspection

of the State frontier between Mongolia and the Russian Federation with a view to more accurately and clearly marking the frontier line, particularly in areas of intensive economic activity by the frontier populations of the parties.

14. The parties will carry out joint and coordinated activities by the law enforcement, frontier and customs bodies and special services of the two countries in order to maintain good order on the Mongolian-Russian frontier, including cooperation to prevent acts of cattle rustling.

15. The parties noted their common or similar approaches to essential current issues, supported an increase in their cooperation in world affairs, and close collaboration with the United Nations and other international organizations. The parties noted with satisfaction the importance of the Millennium Summit, the decisions of which clearly emphasized the enduring significance of the Charter of the United Nations, the central role of the United Nations in the maintenance of international peace and security, and in the peaceful resolution of conflicts, and the importance of strengthening the foundations of international law. They consider that the challenges of the twenty-first century can be met only through the collective efforts of the international community to build a non-confrontational, stable and democratic legal order, taking into account national characteristics and the uniqueness of all peoples, and the wealth of national cultures and traditions.

16. The parties are in favour of enhancing the effectiveness and competence of the United Nations as the only international organization having the principal responsibility for ensuring peace and security. Mongolia and the Russian Federation will promote the Organization's transformation into the key instrument for the collective management of international relations. Mongolia and the Russian Federation have an interest in enhancing the effectiveness of the peacemaking machinery of the United Nations, regard political and diplomatic methods of crisis resolution as a priority and

affirm their commitment to the principles of the primacy of international law. At the same time, the parties support the proposal of the Secretary-General of the United Nations concerning the need to move "from a culture of reaction to a culture of prevention" of armed conflicts. Mongolia and the Russian Federation will contribute to the implementation of the United Nations Millennium Declaration. They are in favour of adapting the United Nations to present-day realities without undermining its underlying principles, and of carrying out a rational reform of the Security Council on the basis of the broadest possible agreement among its members on all key aspects.

17. The parties exchanged opinions on the problem of globalization. They consider that the process of globalization is a fact of life with undoubted positive aspects which offer further opportunities for socio-economic progress and a broadening of human contacts. At the same time, serious efforts by the world community are essential in order to overcome new dangers to which globalization gives rise and which, in many cases, entail a widening of the differences in the level of well-being between the rich and the developing countries.

18. The parties welcome the affirmation, at the 2000 Review Conference of the Parties to the Treaty on the Non-Proliferation of Nuclear Weapons, of the obligation of nuclear-weapon States to take practical steps to ensure systematic and consistent efforts to achieve nuclear disarmament in accordance with article VI of the Treaty. The parties affirmed their commitment to strengthening the regime for the nonproliferation of weapons of mass destruction, expressed the hope that all States would accede to the Treaty on the Non-Proliferation of Nuclear Weapons, the Comprehensive Nuclear-Test-Ban Treaty and the Convention on the Prohibition of Chemical Weapons, and that negotiations on the prohibition of the production of fissionable material for nuclear weapons would be successful, and indicated the importance of complying with generally recognized international standards in carrying out national missile programmes.

19. Mongolia and the Russian Federation are in favour of further strengthening strategic and regional stability and attach importance to the early entry into force and full implementation of the START II Treaty and the conclusion of the START III Treaty, together with the retention and strengthening of the 1972 Anti-Ballistic Missile Treaty as the cornerstone of strategic stability, and the basis for further reductions in nuclear weapons. Mongolia supports the efforts of the Russian Federation to prevent revision of the 1972 Anti-Ballistic Missile Treaty and expresses its concern at plans to deploy national or closed, bloc-based anti-ballistic missile systems. The implementation of such plans would have disastrous consequences for international peace and might lead to a resumption of the arms race from which the developing countries would be the first to suffer.
20. The Russian Federation affirms its commitment to the joint declaration by the five nuclear-weapon States on guarantees for the security of Mongolia in connection with its non-nuclear status. The Mongolian side expressed its appreciation to the Russian side for its efforts to confirm the non-nuclear status of Mongolia and to broaden international recognition thereof. The parties support the efforts of the countries of Central Asia to create in that region a nuclear-weapon-free zone and consider that, in conjunction with the non-nuclear status of Mongolia, those efforts facilitate the realization of the goals of strengthening the nuclear non-proliferation regime in the continent of Asia.
21. Mongolia supports the initiatives of Russian Federation President Vladimir Putin, on the holding, under the auspices of the United Nations, of an international conference on the prevention of the militarization of outer space next spring in Moscow in connection with the fortieth anniversary of the first space flight, and also concerning the non-utilization of enriched uranium and pure plutonium in peaceful nuclear power generation.
22. Mongolia and the Russian Federation are in favour of closely coordinating the efforts of both countries on

questions of peace, security and cooperation in the Asia-Pacific region. They take a positive view of the role of the ASEAN Regional Forum and express their intention to make a worthwhile contribution to its work. Full support was expressed for the official and informal structures for dialogue established within the Asia-Pacific region, and their importance for giving further impetus to multilateral activities to address current problems of regional security and cooperation was emphasized. The Russian Federation supports Mongolia's aspiration to become a member of the Asia-Pacific Economic Cooperation. The parties noted especially the lack of any inter-State mechanism for security and cooperation questions in North-East Asia and expressed their support for increased dialogue through all channels with a view to its establishment. Mongolia and the Russian Federation welcome the outcome of the inter-Korean summit meeting held in Pyongyang from 13 to 15 June 2000 and hope that the process of reconciliation and cooperation on the Korean peninsula will develop further. They are convinced that the maintenance of peace and stability on the Korean peninsula is a major precondition for stability in North-East Asia and in the Asia-Pacific region as a whole. In that context, they were opposed to any unilateral or multilateral actions that might give rise to mutual mistrust between States in that part of the world.

23. The Russian side informed the Mongolian side about the aims, tasks and activities of the Shanghai Forum as an organization open to broad-based international cooperation. The Mongolian side expressed interest in the work of the Forum and said that it would look into the possibility of becoming involved in its work in some form.

24. The parties confirm their aspiration to join forces to oppose international terrorism, religious extremism and national separatism, which threaten regional security, stability and development, and also such forms of criminal activity as illicit trafficking in arms and narcotics and illegal migration.

25. The parties affirm that the Declaration is not directed against any other State or group of States, or against their rights.
26. Russian Federation President Putin expressed appreciation for the cordial welcome received in Ulaanbaatar and invited Mongolian President Bagabandi to visit the Russian Federation at a time convenient to him. The invitation was gratefully accepted.

Ulaanbaatar, 14 November 2000

[Signed] N. **Bagabandi**
President of Mongolia

[Signed] V. V. **Putin**
President of the Russian Federation

APPENDIX IV

Security Assurances for Mongolia

Statement by Mr. john D. Holum, United States Under Secretary of State for Arms Control and International Security, on behalf of France, the People's Republic of China, the Russian Federation, the United Kingdom of Great Britain and Northern Ireland, and the United States of America, in the United Nations First Committee General Debate.

(5 October 2000, New York)

Mr. Chairman,

I am taking this floor on behalf of France, the People's Republic of China, the Russian Federation, the United Kingdom of Great Britain and Northern Ireland, and the United States of America.

It gives me pleasure to announce that our five countries have reached agreement on the text of a Statement concerning security assurances for Mongolia as regards nuclear weapons. With your permission, I would now like to read out the text of this Statement in order to place it on the official record of this Committee.

May I quote:

Statement on Security Assurances in Connection With Mongolia's Nuclear-Weapon-free Status

France, the People's Republic of China, the Russian Federation, the United Kingdom of Great Britain and Northern Ireland, and the United States of America,

Welcoming the declaration by Mongolia of its nuclear-weapon-free status,

Taking into account Mongolia's status as a non-nuclear-weapon state party to the Treaty on the Non-Proliferation of Nuclear Weapons, as well as its unique geographic status,

Welcoming Mongolia's policies of developing peaceful, friendly and mutually beneficial relations with the States of the region and other States,

Confirm the following:

1. France, the People's Republic of China, the Russian Federation, the United Kingdom of Great Britain and Northern Ireland, and the United States of America reaffirm their commitment to Mongolia to cooperate in the implementation of UN General Assembly resolution 55/77D of December 4, 1998 with respect to Mongolia's Nuclear-Weapon-Free Status, in accordance, with the principles of the Charter of the United Nations.
2. France, the People's Republic of China, the Russian Federation, the United Kingdom of Great Britain and Northern Ireland, and the United States of America reaffirm their commitment to seek immediate United Nations Security Council action to provide assistance to Mongolia, as a non-nuclear-weapon state party to the Treaty on the Non-Proliferation of Nuclear Weapons, in accordance with the provisions of UN Security Council resolution 984 of April 11, 1995, if Mongolia should

become a victim of an act of aggression or an object of a threat of aggression in which nuclear weapons are used.

3. France, the People's Republic of China, the Russian Federation, the United Kingdom of Great Britain and Northern Ireland, and the United States of America reaffirm, in the case of Mongolia, their respective unilateral negative security assurances as stated in their declarations issued on 5 and 6 April 1995 and referred to in UN Security Council resolution 984 of April 11, 1995.
4. The People's Republic of China and the Russian Federation recall and confirm the legally-binding commitments undertaken by them with respect to Mongolia through the conclusion of bilateral treaties with Mongolia regarding these matters.

Mr. Chairman, this Statement was prepared by our five countries on the basis of Mongolia's status as a non-nuclear state party in standing as regards the Nuclear Non-Proliferation Treaty. We believe that the unique geographic status of Mongolia made it appropriate for our five countries to provide security assurances in this way since Mongolia is unable to obtain the security assurances that are normally provided by protocols to nuclear-weapon-free zone treaties.

Having joined consensus on UN General Assembly Resolution 53/77D concerning Mongolia's International Security and Nuclear-Weapon-Free Status, the five nuclear-weapon states were pleased to work out an arrangement to provide these security assurances. It is our belief that the Statement I just read into the record fully meets this need. We also believe that our actions further strengthen the NPT by demonstrating our flexibility in responding to the security concerns of NPT non-nuclear-weapon states. In this regard, the nuclear-weapon states note that Mongolia's situation does not pertain to any other state.

The Statement is not eligible for registration under Article 102 of the UN Charter. We wish to state clearly for the record, however, that the five nuclear-weapon states stand fully behind the assurances provided in the Statement.

With the issuance of this Statement, our five countries believe that we have fully carried out the commitment to Mongolia that we undertook as nuclear-weapon states, consistent with the terms of UNGA Resolution 53/77D.

Mr. Chairman, our five countries plan to ask the President of UN General Assembly and the UN Security Council to circulate this Statement as an official document of their respective bodies. In addition, we will arrange for the Statement to be circulated as an official document of the Conference on Disarmament.

Bibliography

Anderson, Jennifer (1997), "The Limits of Sino-Russian Strategic Partnership", *Adelphi Paper*, No. 315.

Atwood, Christopher P. (1999), "Sino-Soviet Diplomacy and Second Partition of Mongolia, 1945-46", in Stephen Kotkin and Bruce A. Elleman, eds. *Mongolia in the Twentieth Century: Landlocked Cosmopolitan,* Armonk, New York: M.E. Sharpe, pp.137-161.

Avarzed, S. (1958), "Foreign Policy of the Mongolian People's Republic," *International Affairs* (Moscow), (10): 39.

Banerjee, D. (1992), "Neither War Nor Peace", *World Focus,* 13 (11-12): 11.

Batbayar, Baabar (2001), "Post-Communist Transition in Mongolia", *Himalayan and Central Asian Studies*, 5(1): 45-54.

Batbayar, Ts. (1993), "Mongolia in 1992: Back to One-Party Rule", *Asian Survey*, 33 (1): 61-66.

Batbayar, Ts. (2003), "Mongolian-Russian Relations in the Past Decade," *Asian Survey*, 43(6): 951-970.

Batbayar, Ts. and Soni, Sharad K. (2007), *Modern Mongolia: A Concise History,* New Delhi: Pentagon Press.

Batjargal, Gunaajav (2010), "Foreign Policy and Development", 10 March, URL: http://www2.jiia.or.jp/en/pdf/kouenkai/2010/100319e-batjargal.pdf

Bayarkhuu, D. (1999), "A New World Order in the Asia-Pacific Region: A Mongolian Perspective," *World Affairs*, 3(4):101.

Bayarkuu, D. (2001), "Mongolia and its Third Neighbours", *Himalayan and Central Asian Studies*, 5(1): 80-90.

Bayarkhuu, D. (2003), "Post Communist Transition and Common Ground: A Mongolian Perspective", *The Mongolian Journal of International Affairs* (Ulaanbaatar) (10): 60-71.

Blagov, Sergei (2005), "Ties between Russia and Mongolia Stall", *Eurasia Daily Monitor*, 3rd February, URL: http://www.jamestown.org/edm/article.php? article_id =2369201.

Blagov, Sergei (2008), "Moscow Seeks to Engage Mongolia Economic Ally", *Eurasia Daily Monitor*, 24th April, URL: http://www.jamestown.org/edm/email-to-friend.php? article_ id =2373002

Bold, R. (1994), "The Changing International Order and Mongolia's Security," The *Mongolian Journal of International Affairs* (Ulaanbaatar), (1): 9-14.

Bold, R.(2000), *The Security of Small State: Option for Mongolia*, Ulaanbaatar: The Institute for Strategic Studies.

Byambasuren, Bayarmagnai (2005), *Challenges Facing Mongolia's Participation in Coalition Military Operation*, Carlisle Barracks: U.S. Army War College.

Campi, Alicia J. (1999), "Moving Mongolian Nomadism intio the 21st Century: Cultural and Ecological Preservation Coupled with Economic Vitality and National Security", *Mongolica* (Ulaanbaatar), 9 (30): 535-567.

Campi, Alicia (2004), "Mongolia in Northeast Asia — The New Realities," URL: http://usmongoliagroup.com/article_northeastasia.htm

Campi, Alicia (2005), "Mongolia in Northeast Asia-The New Realties", *The Mongolian Journal of International Affairs (*Ulaanbaatar), (12): 46-64

Chuluunbat, Zolbayar (2006), "Mongolia", *International Comparisons of Taxation in Developing Countries*, URL: http://www.ic.keio.ac.jp/en/download/jjwbgsp/2006/4_Mongolia.pdf

Dashpurev, D. and S.K. Soni (1992), *Reign of Terror in Mongolia*, New Delhi: South Asian Publishers.

Dorsey, M.A. (2001), "The International Mongolian Economy: The Transition from 1990 to 2000", URL: http://www.hometown.aol.com/dorsenjc/documents/Mongolia economy.doc

Dugersuren, M. (1994), "Changing Mongolia in a New Environment", The *Mongolian Journal of International Affairs* (Ulaanbaatar), No. 1, pp.15-22.

Enkhbayar, Nambaryn (2008), "Mongolia's Foreign Policy: Efforts towards Regional Peace and Security", Speech delivered at the Center for Strategic and International Studies, Washington DC, USA, *The Mongolian Journal of Strategic Studies*, Ulaanbaatar, No.2, 8th February, pp. 6-10.

Enkhsaikhan, J. (1995), "Mongolia's Security Policy: Regional and International Aspects," *The Mongol Messenger*, 18 (210), 14 July.

Enkhsaikhan, J. (2000a), "Mongolia's Nuclear-Weapon-Free Status: Concept and Practice", *Asian Survey* (Berkeley), Vol. 40, No. 2, March-April, p. 359.

Enkhsaikhan, J., (2000b) "Single State NWFZ: From Concept to Practice", *The Mongolian Journal of Strategic Studies*, (2): 17-21.

Eudin, Xenia Joukoff and Robert C. North (1957), *Soviet Russia and the East, 1920-1927: A Documentary Survey,* Stanford:Stanford University Press.

Ewing, T. (1980), .*Between the Hammer and the Anvil?*: *Chinese and Russian Policies in Outer Mongolia, 1911-1921*, Bloomington, Indiana University, Research Institute for Inner Asian Studies.

Galina Yaskina (1998), "Russian-Mongolian Relations: Reality and Outlook", *Far Eastern Affairs*, 5: 32-39.

Garver, John (1988), *Sino-Soviet Relations, 1937–1945: The Diplomacy of Chinese Nationalism.* Oxford: Oxford University Press.

Glenn E. Curtis, ed. (1996), .*Russia: A Country Study*. Washington: GPO for the Library of Congress, URL: http://countrystudies.us/russia/86.htm.

Government of Mongolia (1998), *Mongolian Defence White Paper, 1997-1998,* Ministry of Defence, Ulaanbaatar.

Government of Mongolia (2000), *Mongolian Foreign Policy Blue Book*, Ministry of External Relations of Mongolia, Ulaanbaatar,

Gunaajav Batjargal, "Foreign Policy and Development," March 10, 2010, URL: http://www2.jiia.or.jp/en/pdf/kouenkai/2010/100319e-batjargal.pdf.

Hodder, Dick and others (1998), *Landlocked States of Africa and Asia*, London: Frankcass publishers.

Holub, Alois (1980), "An Introduction to Problems of Economic Development in the CMEA Countries", *Global Economic Review*, 9 (2): 37 – 64.

Hulan, Hashbat (1994), "Mongolia's Political Transformation: Observations and Comparisons", *The Mongolian Journal of International Affairs,* (1): 28-37.

Hyer, Eric A. (2005), "Haunted by History: China and its Northwestern Neighbours", *Historia Actual Online*, (7): 83-92, URL: http://www.historia-actual.org/Publicaciones/index.php/haol/article/viewFile/102/93.

Ian Jeffries (2007), *Mongolia: A Guide to Economic and Political Developments*, New York: Routledge

Korsun, Georges and Peter Mirrell (1995), "Politics and Economics of Mongolia's Privatisation Program", *Asian Survey*, 35(5): 472-486.

Kotkin, Stephen and Bruce Elleman, (eds.) (1999), *Mongolia in the Twentieth Century: Landlocked Cosmopolitan*, Armonk, NY: M.E. Sharpe.

Kyodo (2001), "Russia Expresses Willingness to Help Mongolia with Military", April 23, URL: http://findarticles.com/p/articles/mi_m0WDQ/is_2001_April_23/ai_73597758.

Lhagvasuren, Nomin (2000), "Russia Seeks to Restore Position in Mongolia as Most Favored Neighbor", *Eurasia Insight*, 17 November, URL: http://www.eurasianet.org/departments/insight/articles/eav111700.shtml.

Li Narangoa (2009), "Mongolia and Preventive Diplomacy: Haunted by History and Becoming Cosmopolitan", *Asian Survey*, 49(2): 358-379.

Liu Xiaoyuan (2006), *Reins of Liberation: An Entangled History of Mongolian Independence, Chinese Territoriality, and Great Power Hegemony, 1911-1950*. Stanford: Stanford University Press.

Magid, Alvin and Richard W. Mansbach (1998),"Mongolian Security in the 21st Century: In Quest of Friends and Partners, not Allies", *The Mongolian Journal of International Affairs*, (5): 10-25.

Maygmar, D. (2008), "New Geopolitical Situation and Defence Policy of Mongolia", *The Mongolian Journal of Strategic Studies*, (2): 68-75.

Metcalf, Lee Kendal (1992), "Centripetal and Centrifugal Forces in the CMEA: Prospects for the Future", *Studies in Comparative Communism*, 25(2): pp123-138.

Moiseev, Leonid (2001), "Relations between Russia and Mongolia Are Warming", *Far Eastern Affairs*, (1): 10-17.

Munh-Orgil, Ts. (2005), Regional Integration Processes and Mongolia", *The Mongolian Journal of International Affairs*, (12): 3-7.

National Statistical Office, *Mongolian Statistical Yearbooks-1986 to 2001*, Ulaanbaatar.

Nelles, Wayne (2000), "Reconciling Human and National Security in Mongolia: A Canadian Perspective", Programme on Canada-Asia Policy Studies, Institute of Asian Research, University of British-Columbia, North Pacific Policy Paper 6.

Nomin Lhagvasuren (2000), "Russia seeks to restore position in Mongolia as most favored neighbor," *Eurasia Insight*, 17 November, URL: http://www.eurasianet.org/departments/insight/articles/eav111700.shtml

Nyamdavaa, O. (2001), "Mongolia-India Relations: Some Perspectives", *Himalayan and Central Asian Studies*, 5(1): 19-32.

Peiran, Wang (2009), "Mongolia's Delicate Balancing Act", *China Security*, 5(2): 32-45.

Rossabi, Morris (2005), *Modern Mongolia: From Khans to Commissars to Capitalists,* Berkeley: University of California Press.

Roy, Olivier (2000), *The New Central Asia* , London and New York: I.B. Tauris.

Rupen, Robert A. (1964) *Mongols of the Twentieth Century,* Bloomington: Indiana University.

Sanders, Alan J.K. (1987), *Mongolia: Politics, Economics and Society,* London: Frances Pinter.

Sanjaasuren, Oyun (2008), "Mongolia's Foreign and Security Policy at the Down of the New Century", *The Mongolian Journal of Strategic Studies*, Ulaanbaatar, (2), 8th February: 11-16.

Shagdar, Enkhbayar (2005), "Mongolia's Foreign Trade, 1985-2003", ERINA Report, March, 62: pp1-36.

Shagdar, Enkhbayar (2007), "Neo-liberal 'Shock Therapy' Policy during Mongolian Economic Transition", ERINA Discussion Paper no. 0703e, Niigata, April, pp.1-15.

Soni, Sharad K. (2001), "Mongolia's Foreign Policy Priorities," *Himalayan and Central Asian Studies*, 5(1): pp55-66.

Soni, Sharad K. (2001), "Mongolia and the Soviet Union: A Study of Political Relations (1921-1990)," in Mahavir Singh, ed., *Asia Annual 2001*, Delhi: Shipra, pp. 41-61.

Soni, Sharad K. (2002), *Mongolia-Russia Relations: Kiakhta to Vladivostok*, Delhi: Shipra Publications and Maulana Abul Kalam Azad Institute of Asian Studies.

Soni, Sharad K. (2003), *Mongolia between Russia and China: Emerging Equation,* Kolkata: Maulana Abdul Kalam Azad Institute of Asian Studies.

Soni, Sharad K. (2004), "Democracy at Work: Parliamentary Elections in Mongolia," *Himalayan and Central Asian Studies*, 8(2-3): 101-120.

Soni, Sharad K. (2005), "Mongolia's Security Concerns in the Post-Cold War Period", in Mahavir Singh, ed., *Building a New Asia*, Delhi: Shipra, pp. 282-294.

Soni, Sharad K. (2006), "India's New Role in East Asia: Implications for Mongolia," *The Mongolian Journal of Strategic Studies*, Ulaanbaatar, No. 13, pp. 34-44.

Soni, Sharad K. (2006), *Mongolia-China Relations: Modern and Contemporary Times*, New Delhi: Pentagon Press.

Soni, Sharad K. (2008a), "Post-Cold War Identity of Mongolia: Strategic Concerns", in P.L. Dash (ed.), *Emerging Asia in Focus: Issues and Problems*, Delhi: Academic Excellence, pp. 415-432.

Soni, Sharad K. (2008b), "Democratic Transition in Mongolia: Achievements and Challenges ahead of 2008 Elections", *Bimonthly Journal of Mongolian and Tibetan Current Situation*, (Taipei, Taiwan), 17(1): 31-55.

Soni, Sharad K. (2009), "The Siberian Republic of Tuva: Linkages with Mongolia", in Suchandana Chatterjee and others (eds.), *Asiatic Russia: Partnerships and Communities in Eurasia*, Delhi: Shipra Publications, pp.101-115.

Soni, Sharad K. (2009), "China's Periphery Policy: Implications for Sino-Mongolian Relations", *India Quarterly*, 65(3): 251-269.

Te-Kuang Chang (1998), "Mongolia: A Country Profile", in Willfried A. Hermann, ed., *Asia's Security Challenges*, New York: Nova Science Publishers, p. 252.

Telford, Sarah (2006), "To What Extent Does Post-1990 Mongolia Pursue an Independent Foreign Policy?", *Bimonthly Journal of Mongolian and Tibetan Current Situation* (Taipei, Taiwan), 15 (3), May: 53-75.

Tumurchuluun, G. (1995), "Mongolia's Foreign Policy Revisited: Its relations with Russia and China in the 1990's, *The Mongolian Journal of International Affairs* (Ulaanbaatar), (2): 44-55.

Tumurchuluun, G. (1999), "Mongolia's Foreign Policy Revisited: Relations with Russia and PRC into the 1990s", in Stephen Kotkin and Bruce A. Elleman, eds., *Mongolia in the Twentieth Century: Landlocked Cosmopolitan*, Armonk, New York: M.E.Sharpe, pp. 277-289.

Tumurchuluun, G. (2001), "Mongolia, Russia and China: The Geopolitical Perspective", *Himalayan and Central Asian Studies*, 5(1): 33-44.

Wachman, Allan M. (2009), *Mongolia's Geopolitical Gambit: Preserving a Precarious Independence While Resisting "Soft Colonialism"*, EAI Fellows Program Working Paper Series 18, Seoul: The East Asia Institute.

Warikoo, K., and Sharad K. Soni, eds. (2010), *Mongolia in the 21st Century: Society, Culture and International Relations*, New Delhi: Pentagon Press.

Wolf, Serge M. (1929), "The People's Republic of Mongolia", *Contemporary Review*, (5): 32-39.

Yaskina, Galina (1998), "Russian-Mongolian Relations: Reality and Outlook", *Far Eastern Affairs*, 5: 37.

Zhao, Zhu-cheng (2005), "Mongolian Economic Security Policies toward Russia, 1990- 2000", *Bimonthly Journal of Mongolian and Tibetan Current Situation* (Taipei, Taiwan), 14 (2): 1-18.

Index

A

Agricultural Production, 64
Asian Security
    Mongolia's importance, 28
Atlanticists Alternative, 43

B

Balanced Distance Policy
    Russia-China, 41
Bilateral military co-operation with Russia, 100
Bilateral ties with Russia
    initiatives, 110
    elements, 114
Border Trade, 77

C

Change of name of Mongolia, 37
China
    dependence /influence, 63
    trade, 63
        ...(1999-2000), 72
    Protests
        -Soviet -Mongol Agreements, 19
    Recognition of Mongolian Independence, 19
    -Russia influence, 20
Chinese Dominance
    impact on relations, 46
CMEA Countries
    trade, 24
Cold War End
    impact, 8
COMECON(CommunistEconomies)
    framework dismantling, 21, 62, 64
        ..impact, 62-64
Comintern's Assistance
    to MPRP, 18
Customs & Excise, 67

D

Darkhan Industrial Sector, 24
Defence Ties
    guiding principles, 9
    Mongolia-Russia, 96, 98
    diversification, 97
Democratisation Movement,21
Draft Foreign Policy
    Concept-1993, 43

E

Economic Assistance (1990s), 24
Elbegdorj, Tsakhia
    (Mongolia President), 113
Equi distant
    / Non- Aligned
        Foreign Policy, 101
Eurasian Alternative, 43

Exports Mongolia, 67,70
..2000, 79
major destinations, 71
to Russia(1999-2000), 75

F

Foreign /Security Policy
..objectives, 8
Foreign Direct Investment (FDI),77-78
Foreign Policy
Post 1990 - Goals, 36
New, 38
..directions,39-40
Foreign Policy
Blue Book(2000), 39
Foreign Trade, 70, 80
Policy objective, 65-66
Free Elections – 1990 (Mongolia), 22
Parties Competing, 22

G

GDP, 64Geo Strategic Concerns, 112
Glasnost and *Perestroika* Policies impact, 8
Great Khural
measures taken by, 37-38
Great/Little Khural
seats -MPRP, 22

H

High Level visits, 45

I

Iltod and Orchilan Baigalalt (Soviet Style Reforms), 8,35
Imitation of Soviet Policies by Mongolia, 17
Import
/Export Figures 1995, 70, 75
from Russia, 69-70,75
(1985-2000)
.. Major Partners, 73
International Financial Institutions
- member of, 66
International Relations, 81

J

Japan trade with
-(1999-2000), 72

K

Khalkhin Gon River Battle
60thAnniversary
Celebrations, 46
Kiakhta Agreement-1915, 16

L

Landlocked Position, 62
Law of Mongolia on
Economic entities
(or Company)-1991, 67
Literacy rates, 108

M

Major trading Partners
trade with, 72
Export-(1990, 2000), 76
Manchu rule
(Mongolia), 16
end, 7
Market Economy
adoption of, 37, 64-65, 67
Modern Mongolia :

A Concise History
-Batbayar & Soni, 26
Modern Mongolia :
From Khans to Commissars
to Capitalists -
Rosabbi,26
Mongolia
geo-strategic location, 7
recognition of
independent status, 7, 19
1921 Revolution,7
Mongolia - Russia
Alliance, 8
Political Relations , 109
Mongolia-Russia Relations
Kiakhta to Vladivostok- Soni (2002), 27
Mongolia : Tryst with
Change & Development - R.C. Sharma, 29
Mongolia
under Soviet Umbrella, 8, 15
..causes, 8
Foreign Security Policy, 8
..objectives,8
Mongolia Domestic
& Foreign Policy, 18, 23
..Soviet Control, 19
Mongolia in the Twentieth Century
: Landlocked Cosmopolitan
-Kotkin and Elleman, 25
Mongolia Military Modernization, 112
Mongolia Reforms
(post 1990s), 21
..Foreign Policy
Changes, 23
Mongolian Economy
Structural Changes,62
Mongolian People's Republic
establishment, 7, 15
Mongolian Peoples Revolutionary
Party(MPRP), 18
Mongolia-Russia
Bilateral trade, 68-69
..Accounting Method, 69
relations , 15
..Literature on, 25-29
..history, 16
Mongolia's Geopolitical Gambit
: Preserving a Precarious
Independence - Wachman,28
Mongolia's Relations with
neighbours, 15
MPRP
Electon victory-1992, 23
Reforms/Changes-1990, 22

N

National Security, 39
concept,65, 112
Nuclear Weapons Free Zone
Status, 93, 95
Declaration, 94

O

Oil Pipeline Project
Siberia to China, 110

P

P - 5 Countries
Security assurance
to Mongolia, 94
Policy Issues
- (Key), 38-39
Political Reforms
Mongolia, 21
-1990-1992, 36
Poor nation rank, 108
Post 1991 Period, 110
Post 2000 Period, 111
Post Soviet Collapse
geo-politics Mongolia ,35-36
Security Strategy, 89
Socio-Economic development, 61-62
Post-2000 Scenario, 78-79
Bilateral trade/relationships
problems, 79
advantages, 80
Potential threats
- countries, 102
Privitasition efforts, 67
Putin Vladimir's visit
-2000, 74, 95, 102
impact, 63
.. on security relations, 99-100

R

Regional and Global Issues, 50
Commanalities-Russia and Mongolia, 51
Restoration of Relations
with Russia, 44, 46
Revolutionary Influence
- Mongolia, 18
Russia
trade with
..(1999-2000), 72
..1991-2001 %age Share, 75
as most favoured neighbour, 109
preference, 68
importance, 68-69
Russia Relations
slow down causes, 42
Reorientation, 63
Russia-Mongolia
Friendship (thinkers in favour of), 54
Russian policy
towards Mongolia, 43

S

Shanghai Five Regional
Grouping, 51
Shock Therapy
Mongolia elements, 61
purpose, 62
Sino-Soviet Rapprochment
Process, 102
Socialism influence
on Mongolia, 18
Socialist Ideology
end-Mongolia, 42
Socio-Economic development
1948-90, 61
Post Soviet Collapse, 61-62
Soviet Aid, 24
Soviet Collapse
impact on Russia, 44

Soviet Domination
/Infiltration
over Mongolia, 8, 15, 17
Channels, 18
Soviet Influence in Mongolia channels, 18
Soviet Troops
Withdrawal, 20
Soviet Union Breakdown -1991
impact, 8
Vladivostok Initiative-Gorbachev's, 8
Soviet Union collapse, 21
impact, 23, 25, 108
Soviet-Mongol Agreements, 19
Soviet-Mongol Gentlemen's
Agreement-1934, 19
Soviet-Mongol Protocol
of Mutual Assistance, 19

T

Tax Simplification, 65
Third Neighbours
economic interests with, 114
Trade Balance (Mongolia)
1999-2001, 68
Trade Cooperation, 111
Turnover, 111
Trade deficit
Countering measures, 67
Trade Liberalization, 66-67
Trade Protocol with Russia, 70
Traditional Balance of Power
Theory(Mongolia), 15
Traffic Constraints, 101
Transit Development
Strategies, 65
Treaty of Friendly Relations
and Cooperation-1993,96,
Truth History and
Politics in Mongolia :
The Memory of Heroes - Kaplouski, 26

U

Ulaanbaatar Declaration -2000, 48-50, 95, 99
on strategic partnership,99-100
on Military Coup, 113
impact on relations, 50
commitments, 52
Ulaanbaatar-Moscow relations
-1991, 25
UN Millenium Summit (2000) Participation, 54
UN resolution on
Mongolia's International Security, 95
US trade with
-(1999-2000), 72
Vladivostok Initiative, 8,38
War on Terror support, 109